THE SUNDAY TIMES

MY BIG IDEA

30 successful entrepreneurs reveal how they found inspiration

Rachel Bridge

KOGAN PAGE

London and Philadelphia

Publisher's note

Every possible effort has been made to ensure that the information contained in this book is accurate at the time of going to press, and the publishers and author cannot accept responsibility for any errors or omissions, however caused. No responsibility for loss or damage occasioned to any person acting, or refraining from action, as a result of the material in this publication can be accepted by the editor, the publisher or the author.

First published in Great Britain and the United States in 2006 by Kogan Page Limited
Reprinted in 2007

Apart from any fair dealing for the purposes of research or private study, or criticism or review, as permitted under the Copyright, Designs and Patents Act 1988, this publication may only be reproduced, stored or transmitted, in any form or by any means, with the prior permission in writing of the publishers, or in the case of reprographic reproduction in accordance with the terms and licences issued by the CLA. Enquiries concerning reproduction outside these terms should be sent to the publishers at the undermentioned addresses:

120 Pentonville Road
London N1 9JN
United Kingdom
www.kogan-page.co.uk

525 South 4th Street, #241
Philadelphia PA 19147
USA

© Rachel Bridge, 2006

The right of Rachel Bridge to be identified as the author of this work has been asserted by her in accordance with the Copyright, Designs and Patents Act 1988.

ISBN-10   0 7494 4626 9
ISBN-13   978 0 7494 4626 0

The views expressed in this book are those of the author, and are not necessarily the same as those of Times Newspapers Ltd.

British Library Cataloguing-in-Publication Data

A CIP record for this book is available from the British Library.

Library of Congress Cataloging-in-Publication Data

Bridge, Rachel.
My big idea : 30 successful entrepreneurs reveal how they found inspiration /
Rachel Bridge.
     p. cm.
"Based on Rachel Bridge's "How I Made It" column in The Sunday Times where they originally appeared in a shortened form during 2004 and 2005. All have been completely revised and updated for inclusion in this book"—P.   .
     ISBN 0-7494-4626-9
     1. Businesspeople—Great Britain—Biography. 2. Executives–Great Britain—Biography. 3. Directors of corporations—Biography. 4. Entrepreneurship—Great Britain—Case studies. I. Title.
HC252.5.A2B75 2006
338'.04092241—dc22   2006008146

Typeset by Saxon Graphics Ltd, Derby
Printed and bound in Great Britain by MPG Books Ltd, Bodmin, Cornwall

Contents

Acknowledgements

I would like to thank all the entrepreneurs for their time and generosity in sharing their experiences for this book.

I would also like to thank Jon Finch and everyone at Kogan Page for their help in making this book a reality.

A big thank you to *The Sunday Times* for its support, especially editor John Witherow, business editor John Waples and managing editor Richard Caseby.

Once again thank you also to Kathleen Herron and Rebecca Chambers for their unfailing enthusiasm and encouragement.

Finally a big thank you to my family and friends, especially Anika and Tanya, for all their help and good advice.

Rachel Bridge
London

The articles in this book were based on Rachel Bridge's 'How I Made It' column in *The Sunday Times* where they originally appeared in a shortened form during 2004 and 2005. All have been completely revised and updated for inclusion in this book.

Photograph of Judy Craymer by Joan Marcus

For Harry

Introduction

Have you ever wondered why you never see shops selling chocolate-covered sprouts? Or cat food that glows in the dark? Or why you can't buy edible cutlery? Well it's probably because they are not very good ideas. Unfortunately it is usually far easier to think up hopeless ideas than good ones. In fact one of the biggest things that deters would-be entrepreneurs from taking the plunge and setting up their own business is the lack of a promising idea.

So what constitutes a good idea? How do you go about looking for one? And when you find one, how do you know if it will be good enough to turn into a successful business?

As the Enterprise Editor of *The Sunday Times* I have spoken to hundreds of successful entrepreneurs about where and how they found the inspiration for their business. This book tells the stories of 30 of them. Their answers will intrigue and inspire you.

The first requirement of a good business idea is that it solves a problem. Indeed Doug Richard, a judge on the BBC television show *Dragons' Den* and founder of research company The Library House, says that the secret to finding potential ideas is to start seeing every problem in life as an opportunity.

He says: 'People walk around being annoyed at how awkward the world is, not realising that in fact they are being presented with a buffet of ideas-in-waiting. Whenever you say to yourself that you are annoyed by something, you should say to yourself, I wonder if there is a better way. And in that lies the genesis of most ideas. Almost all great ideas come out of transforming a problem into a solution. As soon as you start looking at all the problems in life as opportunities, then you will find yourself with many potential ideas to choose from.'

Will King, for example, decided to start making shaving oil because he had sensitive skin and was fed up with getting razor burn every time he shaved. When his girlfriend suggested he use oil on his skin before shaving he discovered to his surprise that it completely solved the problem. From there it was a short step to realising that other people who suffered while shaving might be interested in his discovery too, and his shaving oil King of Shaves was born.

A good business idea does not have to be complicated. Sally Preston did not have time to spend hours in the kitchen preparing home-made food for her daughter so she decided to make nutritious baby food which was ready-frozen in ice-cube trays. That way busy parents could instantly defrost as much or as little as they needed to feed their baby yet still feel confident that they were providing their baby with a healthy meal. Her Babylicious products are now stocked by supermarkets across the country.

Emma Harrison, a business mentor and founder of A4e, a training and employment organisation, says: 'The best ideas are the simplest ideas. They are the ones that come from people using a product or service which is inadequate and deciding they can do it better.'

In fact some of the best ideas are the simple ones that make you want to thump your head in frustration and say, 'Now why didn't I think of that?' Take the Post-it note. Or the wind-up radio. Or those little corrugated cardboard sleeves you get in Starbucks to stop you burning your hand on the cup. All are brilliant ideas. All are maddeningly simple. All have made someone somewhere a lot of money.

Your idea must also be practicable. If you need to spend years and years researching and developing your concept into a workable product or service then the chances are high that someone else will beat you to it. And that you will run out of money before you get there. When it comes to getting new ideas out into the market place, speed is of the essence. Ask yourself, 'How hard would it be to do? And do I really have the skills and know-how to make this happen?'

However, the most important requirement of a good business idea is that there is a market for it. That means there must be enough people out there who are willing to buy your product or service to make it worth your while.

Harrison says: 'So many people sit squirreling away in their garden sheds dreaming up new products or services but they have no idea how they are ever going to link themselves to the market place. They are earnest but misguided. There is no point creating a product or service unless someone wants to buy it. You first have to go out there and talk to people about your product and get their reactions to it. Entrepreneurial activity that really works is when you identify a gap in the market first – and then develop something to fill it.'

By doing this you can also work out how much someone would be willing to pay for your product or service. Richard says: 'Find out what it costs people NOT to have your idea in their lives. It may not necessarily be money, it could be time, effort, quality of life or something else. The cost to them of living with the problem equals the value to them of you removing the problem.'

When Martyn Dawes started up his Coffee Nation business, providing coffee machines to corner shops, he initially offered vending machines which used instant coffee and powdered milk. But sales were sluggish and after talking to potential customers he realised that they were not buying his coffee because it was no better than what they could make themselves at work. What people really wanted was high quality coffee made from freshly ground beans and real milk. So Dawes completely changed the approach of the business and his company now sells 750,000 cups of coffee every month.

Daniel Ronen, director of Portman Business Consultancy, says: 'It is fantastic to have a wonderful concept but if you can't take it to market then it is not worth a penny. The issue of commerciality is where most people fall down. They come up with this wonderful new idea for a product or service but they don't know how to commercialise it and that is when things start to collapse.'

In order for an idea to be an astoundingly good idea, it also needs to have wings. In other words, how big is the potential opportunity? The way to find out that, says Richard, is to start talking to the people who might want to buy your product or service.

He says: 'Go and talk to as many prospective customers as you can. If you want to open a sandwich shop in a specific place then you should be finding ways to talk to people who might buy sandwiches at that spot. You can learn so much that way. Often people say they want to wait until they have got further with starting up their business before they start talking to people about their idea. But if you talk to a prospective customer you will learn most of what you need to know to determine whether the idea is good or bad.'

When Stephen Waring wanted to start up his lawn treatment service the first thing he did was go round knocking on doors on the local housing estate to see if people would be interested in paying to have well-tended green lawns. And Guy Schanschieff spent years talking to parents while collecting and washing their babies' dirty nappies before starting up his own reusable nappy business, Bambino Mio.

So where do you start looking for ideas? The first place to start your search is in your own personal environment. As with some of the people in this book, your idea could spring from something that is missing in your own life.

Will Ramsay loved going to art galleries but was intimidated by the frosty attitude of the people working in them. He decided there had to be a friendlier, less intimidating way of buying art than from individual art galleries so he started up the Affordable Arts Fair, where people could feel comfortable wandering around to look at the paintings and the prices are clearly shown so they do not have to ask.

Then again your idea might come from spotting a more efficient way of doing things in your work environment. Paul Stanyer had spent many years working for holiday companies in resorts around the Mediterranean. He started up his business HolidayTaxis.com after realising that holiday makers arriving at the airport would probably prefer to have a pre-ordered taxi waiting for them to take them direct to their hotel instead of spending hours on a transfer bus as it went round all the resorts dropping people off.

Some people in this book found their big idea by turning conventional wisdom on its head. Karen Darby decided that instead of cold-calling customers to persuade them to switch energy suppliers, she would set up a comparison service called Simply Switch so that the customers themselves would want to pick up the phone and make the call to see if they could get a better deal.

Other people in this book found the inspiration for their business by seeing a successful idea in action overseas and deciding it might work in the UK too. David Sanger started selling high quality hot dogs in the UK after seeing how popular they were in Copenhagen.

Other people's ideas grew out of a hobby or interest. Mark Leatham loved hunting and fishing as a child and grew up surrounded by good food. He has now built a business that specialises in seeking out little-known good food from around the world.

Harrison says: 'You can't just sit in your room in isolation and come up with an idea. You have to be out there travelling, talking, reading, watching, listening, experiencing. It is then that you will spot something that you don't like and decide to do it better.'

Unfortunately, despite your best efforts there is no guarantee you will stumble upon a winning idea first time. Most of the entrepreneurs in this book took several attempts at finding a successful idea before they hit the big time. David Salisbury, for example, started out making work benches before switching to making conservatories. And even when you have got the basic concept right, it can still take a change of direction to turn it into one that will really fly. Helen Colley spent years cooking fantastic main courses and puddings for special events through her outside catering business, but it was only when she hit upon selling her puddings direct to the public through shops that her business Farmhouse Fare really took off.

Indeed, some ideas take years to become reality. It took Judy Craymer 10 years of hard work and persuasion before she was able to turn her idea of creating a musical using Abba songs into reality. Happily, the effort paid off in the end – her musical *Mamma Mia* has so far taken more than US $1 billion at the box office.

The good news is that there is no shortage of potentially fabulous ideas around just waiting to be discovered – and nor are we ever likely to run out of them. Richard says: 'Every innovation spawns 10 innovations. If you view the world as a series of unsolved problems and inconveniences then that means there will be a continual flow of ideas.'

The truth is that inspiration for that winning business idea is all around you. You just have to look carefully and spot it before someone else does.

So what are you waiting for? Read this book and get ready for inspiration to strike.

1

Martyn Dawes
Founder of Coffee Nation

Being around Martyn Dawes when he is getting enthusiastic about something can be a rather alarming experience.

He says: 'I have a habit of making a very strange noise when I get very excited. It sounds a bit like the noise Al Pacino makes in the film *Scent of a Woman*. It invariably makes people jump, particularly if they are on the phone.'

Dawes has much to be excited about right now. His company Coffee Nation now sells 750,000 cups of coffee from its self-service machines every month and is expected to have sales of around £24 million in 2006.

Born in Coventry, Dawes was adopted at six weeks old by a couple who were unable to have children of their own. He says: 'I was their whole focus and a lot of love and encouragement came my way.'

But Dawes was always restless, caused partly, he now thinks, by uncertainty over his origins. 'I wanted to get out there and show what I could do. I had a need to prove myself. I think it was a way of compensating for not knowing where I came from.'

He was so keen to get started that he dropped out of college halfway through his A levels at the age of 17 to work for a local foundry where his father worked. In his spare time he took flying lessons and dreamed of becoming a pilot. But his dream was shattered when he discovered he was colour blind. So at the age of 21 he got a job with Massey Ferguson, the tractor maker.

He did well but after a year he met his future wife, Trudi, and decided to move to London to be with her. He set up on his own as a self-employed management consultant for engineering companies and soon discovered he had a knack for it.

He says: 'When you are 23 you have a wonderful sort of arrogance and inbuilt self-confidence because you haven't had the experience that says you could get your fingers burned.'

Within six months he had started up his own consultancy, and soon his wife, who worked in human resources, joined him.

The consultancy did well, but by the time Dawes was 28 he was getting restless. He says: 'I have got a very low boredom threshold and I realised that consulting was not really what I loved doing. I could see that businesses interested me more than consulting did.'

So he took £50,000 out of the consultancy business and started looking around for inspiration to start up a business of his own. It was, however, harder than he thought. He says: 'It is very hard to find something when you don't know what you are looking for. I would get knots in my stomach because I was so scared.'

He briefly considered buying a clothing company that had gone bust, and also looked into the idea of opening a chain of workplace children's nurseries. He says: 'I looked at everything. I literally had a blank sheet of paper in front of me.'

One day he read an article in a newspaper about a company which was doing well by putting photocopiers into newsagents and corner shops. It got him thinking.

He says: 'I liked the idea of a business model in which you could generate a little bit of revenue from lots of different places. That way you would not be reliant on any one of them too much and would never be really exposed to one customer. And you would be using the foot traffic of people already going into those stores.'

Fact file

Date of birth: 14 January 1968

Marital status: divorced with one child

Qualifications: BA (Hons) business studies degree from South Bank Polytechnic

Interests: socialising, sports cars, taking flying trapeze lessons

Personal philosophy: 'Never ever give up.'

He decided to visit the United States in search of inspiration, starting in New York and then heading for Minneapolis, which at the time had the biggest shopping mall in the world. While he was there Dawes initially toyed with the idea of becoming the UK franchisee for a frozen yoghurt business. But at the last minute he realised that it might not be such a good idea because the sun does not shine much in England. He was also entranced by a restaurant called The Screening Room which contained several tiny cinemas for groups of friends to watch films together. But he quickly realised that to open something similar in the UK would involve a huge investment of capital.

His big idea eventually came to him when he was standing in a local New York convenience store. He noticed that large numbers of people were coming in simply to buy a cup of coffee to take away and realised that there might be a similar demand for takeaway coffee in the UK too. Following the photocopier business model he had read about, he would install instant coffee machines in corner shops and give a percentage of the money earned from the machine to the shop owner.

Back home in the UK, Dawes got to work. He persuaded four independent corner shops to take his machines, which he filled with instant coffee powder and powdered milk. But he quickly discovered that not many people actually wanted to buy instant coffee from a machine in a grubby little shop.

He says: 'I remember walking through Peckham thinking what the hell am I doing? It was the wrong product in the wrong shops in the wrong location.'

So he started putting his instant coffee machines into larger convenience stores such as Spar and Alldays. But by 1997 he realised that the product and the location were still wrong. He says: 'I was selling 50–60 cups a week but that was never going to spin the wheel.'

His personal life also took a nosedive. He and his wife separated and Dawes found himself sleeping on friends' floors.

Then one day he was standing near one of his machines talking to customers when one of them said something that hit a nerve. Dawes says: 'The man said to me, "Why would I spend 59p on a cup of coffee when I can go back to the office and put the kettle on? If you want to sell me something in a store like this it has got to really excite me."'

Dawes suddenly realised the answer to his business problems was to provide machines that made real coffee with fresh milk. So he persuaded a couple of manufacturers to lend him a few genuine espresso machines to try out, and quickly saw sales improve. 'It was a eureka moment. I felt fantastic.'

Unfortunately, his euphoria did not last long. By this time he had come to the end of his £50,000 and had no money left.

He went to see an insolvency practitioner at his accountant's firm for advice on winding up the company. But while he was there he happened to bump into an adviser who thought he might be able to find investors for Dawes' business.

So Dawes quickly wrote a business plan and was given the chance to pitch at a forum for investors. By the end of the day he had secured investment of £100,000 in return for 20 per cent of the company's equity. That unlocked the door to a £90,000 bank loan – and Dawes was back in business. He began to find better sites for his machines and two years later managed to raise £4 million from venture capitalists to invest in growing the company, leaving him with a 25 per cent stake.

His Coffee Nation gourmet coffee stations are now in over 400 outlets including Tesco stores and Welcome Break motorway services, where they serve real espresso coffee made with fresh milk and fresh coffee beans. Dawes has also installed his machines in Odeon Cinemas and W H Smith outlets in airports and stations, and is planning to expand throughout mainland Europe.

Now 38, Dawes is immensely proud of what he has achieved. He says: 'I was tempted to give up many times. But if you do and somebody else makes it with your idea, you have got the rest of your life to kick yourself and think of what might have been.'

He credits his ex-wife Trudi with much of his success and giving him the drive to succeed, saying: 'She was and continues to be an enormous source of inspiration to me. When I first became self-employed at the age of 23 she could see in me what I couldn't see in myself. I would not be where I am today, and I wouldn't have the confidence or the self-belief without her.'

Dawes has also succeeded in resolving much of his restless search for his true identity. Four years ago he finally met his birth mother for the first time. To his surprise he discovered she is something of an entrepreneur herself and runs her own corporate gift business.

He says: 'When I met her I could see exactly the same traits in her as in me, and it has enabled me to relax a bit with myself. I had always thought, why am I like this, why do I always want more? And now I know.'

2

Judy Craymer
Creator of Mamma Mia

When Judy Craymer was a child she was convinced that her future career would involve horses in some way. Brought up in a middle class home in North London, she had a horse of her own and spent her teenage years going to horse shows every weekend and riding horses for other owners.

She also got her first taste of the theatre while growing up. Her parents, a solicitor and a nurse, were keen theatre goers and would often take her and her younger brother to see shows in the West End. She says: 'I am forever grateful to them for that. It was a huge treat. The first musical I saw was *Oliver*. And it was a big experience going to the Haymarket and seeing *The Merchant of Venice* with Sir Ralph Richardson. We would also take picnics to the open air opera in Holland Park.'

The visits to the West End evidently made a big impression because at the age of 18 Craymer suddenly changed her mind about pursuing a career with horses and decided that she wanted to go to drama school instead. She says: 'One of my horses became very ill and I just thought that's it, I am going to the Guildhall School of Music.'

Right from the start, however, she knew that she did not want to become an actress, preferring to work behind the scenes. She got a place to study stage management and loved it. She says: 'I was just in love with what I was doing there. I got completely involved with everything and it became my social life as much as studying.'

After graduating she got a job as an assistant stage manager at the Haymarket theatre in Leicester. Several jobs in stage management followed, until at the age of 22 she landed a job in London as assistant stage manager for the original production of the musical *Cats*.

A year later she became assistant to theatre producer Tim Rice. While she was there she met Bjorn Ulvaeus and Benny Andersson, two of the members of the Swedish pop group Abba. The group had just disbanded and the two of them were writing the music for Rice's musical *Chess*.

It was a pivotal moment. Craymer says: 'I was never a huge Abba fan as a teenager, but after meeting Bjorn and

Benny I became hooked. I thought bloody hell, these were the men who wrote "Dancing Queen".'

After five years she left her job with Rice to work in the film industry as a director's assistant, working on films such as *White Mischief* and *Madame Souzatska*. But her new-found interest in Abba refused to go away. Now in her mid-30s, she started spending hours on end sitting on the floor of her flat listening to old Abba records. Eventually she decided she wanted to make a film that told a story using their songs and she started making tapes of how the songs would fit together.

Craymer had stayed in touch with Ulvaeus because he kept a horse at his house in England which she would occasionally exercise for him. So one day she plucked up the courage to mention her idea of making a film based on their music. He and Andersson were encouraging, albeit rather bemused. Craymer says: 'They patted me on the head and said see you next year.'

In the end, however, turning her idea into a realistic project took rather longer than a year. In fact Craymer continued to think about how to turn her Abba project into reality for the next 10 years while taking jobs in the film and television industry. When it seemed as though pursuing her Abba idea was leading nowhere, she tried to turn her attention to other

Fact file

Date of birth: 16 April 1958

Marital status: single

Qualifications: Diploma from Guildford School of Music

Interests: horse riding, theatre

Personal philosophy: 'Make people believe in what you are doing.'

ideas. She says: 'I had lots of other ideas. I was working very hard trying to find projects.'

But her Abba dream refused to go away. She kept coming back to it and finally in 1995 she had her big idea. She suddenly realised her idea would work much better as a musical than a film. Rejuvenated, she went back to talk to Ulvaeus and Andersson. They told her that if she could come up with a good story then they would consider giving her the rights to use their songs.

Encouraged by their response, Craymer gave up her job, found someone to write the script with and got to work. The two of them decided that the musical should tell the story of a mother and a daughter.

She found little support from her friends however. She says: 'Everyone thought I was crazy. They said that Abba was so passé, and that I should get over it. No one could understand.'

She started to gather people around her to help but as the project gained momentum the tension started to mount. Craymer says: 'I still didn't have the rights to the songs and I knew that at any moment Bjorn and Benny could jump ship. It was a white knuckle ride because by then I'd started having to pay people. It kept me so focused. Also I knew that they had not had a particularly good experience working on the musical *Chess*, and that if my project was going to have backstage squabbles and unhappy people they would just walk away.'

Craymer also had to start spending her own money on lawyers' fees, flying overseas for meetings and hiring a creative team to work on the project. By 1997 she had run up a £20,000 overdraft and had to sell her flat. She says: 'I think I just numbed myself to it.'

But her persistence eventually paid off. By the end of 1997 she had finally secured Ulvaeus and Andersson's agreement to use their songs and set up her own company with them to hold the rights to the show. After a year of negotiations and meetings she also managed to persuade Abba's record producer Polygram to finance half the £3-million cost of putting the show on London – and even got them to advance her £300,000 to workshop the show, which was to be called *Mamma Mia*. Ulvaeus and Andersson helped persuade a Swedish bank to invest the rest of the money they needed.

Mamma Mia finally opened in London's West End in April 1999 and the show was an instant success, selling out every night for weeks in advance. And that was just the start. *Mamma Mia* has since grossed over a billion US dollars at the box office, has opened in more than 120 major cities and has been seen by 24 million people worldwide.

In 2005 Craymer's company Littlestar, in which she has a 50 per cent share, had a turnover of over £23 million. All the creative team involved in the show have become million-aires and Craymer herself currently earns an estimated £4 million a year from the show, amassing her a personal fortune of an estimated £67 million. Craymer says: 'I still can't really quite believe it. I never knew we had such a hit on our hands. I just wanted to make it work.'

Now aged 48, she thinks the secret of her success has been her sheer determination not to give up. 'You have to make people believe in what you are doing. I was so passionate about it that when someone at one of the meetings suggested we put the show off I just shouted "No you can't do this, it has to happen."'

She thinks that although someone might have several ideas for projects, the key to being successful is to choose just one of them and then to focus on it completely. She says: 'You have to concentrate on something to achieve some-thing. This has taken every fibre of my focus and concentra-tion for a number of years. *Mamma Mia* is my life. It is a complete obsession.'

The rewards have been immense, and not just in financial terms. She says: 'One of my ambitions was never having to work for somebody else again, I wanted the freedom to create projects on my own and not to have to go cap in hand to people. And that is what I have got.'

3

Stephen Waring
Founder of Green Thumb

Stephen Waring's entrepreneurial instincts kicked in early. At the age of 14 he started making money in his spare time by framing old prints and selling them at local fetes. He says: 'I would find pictures in the *Illustrated London News* which were of the local area and then frame them. I was always interested in ways of making a few bob.'

One of five children, Waring was born in Wirral, Liverpool, but when he was four years old his family moved to North Wales. He was a high achiever at school and at the age of 10 he was moved up a year.

His father was a sales director for an insulation company. By the time Waring was 16 he had begun canvassing potential customers for the firm his father worked for by knocking on doors and telling people that they could get a government grant to help them insulate their lofts. He found he was good at it and so when he left school at 17 Waring decided to start up his own loft insulation company.

Despite getting three A levels, which he took a year early, he never considered going to university. He says: 'I always

felt that you don't necessarily need qualifications to take advantage of a business opportunity. And I took the view that if I wanted to be successful then I could do it myself.'

Waring quickly generated so much business providing loft insulation that he persuaded his older brother to come and help him. When his brother got married to an American girl in 1985 Waring flew to the United States for the wedding. While he was there he had his big idea. He started talking to the bride's uncle, who owned a lawn treatment company and when he discovered that 24 per cent of US households regularly paid someone to have their lawns treated, Waring was hooked. He says: 'People would pay for the company to come round to their homes seven or eight times a year to fertilise the lawn and get rid of the weeds and reduce the problem of insects. And they would pay for that year in year out. I thought it was an interesting concept.'

By the time he got back home Waring had decided to forget about loft installation and start a lawn treatment company of his own. His parents were not convinced that anyone in the UK would pay to have a green lawn but, undaunted, Waring started researching his idea.

He says: 'I went to the local library and looked through every *Yellow Pages* in the country under garden services to see whether somebody else was already doing it. Nobody was. Here was a service that millions of people in the United States used – it was bigger than double glazing – and yet nobody did it in Britain.'

He spent the next six months trying to recreate the green lawns he had seen in the United States. First he read every bit of information he could lay his hands on, then he went round local housing estates studying the difference between lawns that were nice and lawns that were not. He says: 'I was struck by the potential to create beautiful lawns because the vast majority of people didn't have them.'

Then he started mixing together fertiliser ingredients such as nitrogen phosphate and potash in a bucket to experiment on his parents' lawn. He says: 'It was trial and error. First I turned my parents' lawn orange and then I turned it black.'

Eventually Waring hit upon a mixture that turned lawns green. He spent £64 getting a thousand leaflets printed advertising his services and distributed them around the

Fact file

Date of birth: 8 October 1965

Marital status: married with two children

Qualifications: three A levels

Interests: studying historical texts

Personal philosophy: 'My business is my slave, not my master.'

housing estates near his home in North Wales. Then he went round knocking on doors. He managed to get 70 customers.

Waring quickly established a routine that involved visiting each lawn four or five times a year to treat people's lawns, effectively turning the business into a year-round service. He says: 'It is important in any industry that there is longevity throughout the year otherwise you are talking about a seasonal business.'

It was, however, initially a challenge starting an industry completely from scratch. He says: 'I wasn't selling a service to people that they were accustomed to, so I had to sell them an idea or a concept. So it wasn't a question of, hello, would you like new windows or doors – I had to explain what we actually did before I could tell them how much it cost. And some of the equipment I started with was fairly basic. The challenge was developing an industry from scratch as opposed to jumping on the bandwagon of somebody else already doing it.'

As word of his amazing green lawns spread, more customers followed. Soon Waring had so much work that he employed his younger brother to help him. He says: 'People were amazed with the results I was getting and they were recommending me to friends and neighbours. Even after one treatment people would notice an incredible difference. Everybody came back for more.'

By 1995 Waring had amassed several thousand regular customers. To cope with the demand he persuaded his brother-in-law to set up a branch of Green Thumb in Warrington. Then he split his operation in North Wales into two so he had three branches of the business.

Then one day Waring was asked by a customer who was moving out of the area if he would sell him a franchise to open a Green Thumb branch of his own in Buckinghamshire. Waring decided that franchising the business would make a lot of sense and so in 1996 he started selling franchises. He now has 113 franchisees and can potentially service 7 million homes in the UK.

Green Thumb currently has 185,000 customers and the average customer pays around £26 for a treatment and has five treatments a year. Franchisees have combined sales of £25 million a year, giving the company annual royalties of £5 million. The company is currently growing at 5 per cent every month.

Waring, however, has no interest in expanding into mowing lawns. He says: 'People ask me that a lot because they see lots of bolt-on opportunities for my business. But anybody can go out and buy a lawn mower and cut somebody's lawn and get paid £7 an hour. We are providing a specialist service. And why would I want to take my eye off the ball by trying to complicate our service by adding other things at the moment? We are still embryonic in our growth.'

Now 40 and married with two sons, Waring says he was always confident Green Thumb would be big. He says: 'When people ask me if I thought my business would be as successful as it has been, I have to say yes, because the industry is huge in America and yet in some ways the English climate is even more conducive to lawn treatment than the climate in America is.'

He put the secret of his success down to self-belief. He says: 'It helps to have a strong personal belief in your own abilities and not to feel insecure because you didn't go to university and get a degree in business studies.'

He is also a believer in always looking at the bigger picture. He says: 'One of things I think has helped to drive the growth of this business is that rather than sitting down and trying to reduce costs by saving a penny here and a penny there, we spend the same amount of money in generating business. That way you can make pounds rather than saving pennies.'

Despite his success, and unlike many other entrepreneurs, Waring is a firm believer in maintaining a healthy work–life balance. He spends only three and a half days a week at work and he and his family spend every winter in Florida.

He says: 'I don't believe in working all hours. It is better to work smart rather than long and hard. Some people say lunch is for wimps – what a load of rubbish. My business is my slave, not my master.' He adds: 'Money doesn't motivate me. But that is not to say that I don't drive a Bentley Continental T2.'

4

Will King

Founder of King of Shaves

When Will King decided he wanted to call his shaving oil King of Shaves, he faced a problem. Using the words 'King of' was deemed to be a laudatory trademark implying that his product was the best, and so was not allowed.

Undaunted, King simply hired a patent attorney and argued his case in the European Patent Court. He won.

King has never been one to give up easily. Brought up in Lowestoft, Suffolk, where both his parents were teachers, he learnt to sail while still at school and soon became passionate about it. By the age of 15 he had become the UK's youngest sailing instructor. He says: 'I was quite introvert at the time and I was not that happy at school because my dad taught there and I took a bit of stick for being a teacher's son. But then I found something that I was really good at.'

His passion for boats led him to apply for a degree place at Southampton University studying ship science and yacht design. But he didn't get the A level grades he needed to get on the course and suddenly found himself adrift. He managed to get a place on a naval engineering course at

polytechnic but while he was away in New Zealand on a gap year the course changed to mechanical engineering, something he had no real interest in. He says: 'It was designing gas turbo engines and my maths wasn't that great so I really had to work very hard at it.'

Things went from bad to worse. He found out that Simon Le Bon, the lead singer with pop band Duran Duran was hiring crew to sail his boat Drum and so King decided to get a place on board and run away to sea. But he got to the boatyard a day too late. He says: 'If I had gone on Thursday afternoon instead of staying for a maths lesson my life would have been completely different. I was absolutely distraught.'

After a few days staying with friends on the Isle of Wight he decided to ring his parents and ask their advice. They told him to go back and finish his degree, so he did. When he graduated in 1987 his parents told him it was time for him to get a job. So with no idea what he wanted to do King applied for a job selling advertising space for a marketing magazine which promised a big salary if he met sales targets. He threw himself into the challenge.

He says: 'I have always believed that persistence is a good value to have so I started making 220 calls a day to have nine effective calls to close two or three deals. It was very eye-opening. I learnt a huge amount. If you didn't put in the volume of the calls you weren't going to get the sales.'

King found he was good at selling and after three months he was offered a job with a conference company selling events. He set himself a target of doubling his salary, learning to drive and buying a flat within his first year. He achieved all three.

But then things started to go wrong. Recession hit and the company he worked for found itself in trouble. King had to make people redundant and was then made redundant himself.

He realised, however, that although people had stopped spending money on conferences, they were still buying small essential items such as batteries and razors. So he decided to find a product he could sell himself. He says: 'I decided that however bad things are people will always

Fact file

Date of birth: 18 August 1965

Marital status: separated with one child

Qualifications: BEng (Hons) in mechanical engineering from Portsmouth Polytechnic

Interests: yachting, collecting antiques, windsurfing, thinking

Personal philosophy: 'Enthuse, exceed, enjoy – enthuse about what you do, try to exceed at it, but above all enjoy it.'

need a product of some sort. And I wanted to be master of my own destiny. So then it was just a matter of deciding which product.'

He soon found that his big idea lay right in front of him. King had always had trouble shaving because he had sensitive skin and the razor would leave his face itchy and bleeding. So one day his girlfriend suggested that he put some bath oil on his skin before shaving and see if it made a difference. It did. He says: 'It felt fantastic. I didn't get any razor burn. I thought if this works for me, it will work for other people.'

Inspired by the discovery, he bought a selection of exotic and essential oils from an aromatherapy shop and mixed them together at home to create a shaving oil. Then he tracked down the supplier and bought large quantities of the oils, funding his venture by taking out a £10,000 loan and borrowing £30,000 from two friends in return for shares in the business.

He says: 'I filled 10,000 bottles by hand at home. It took me two weeks.' He initially thought about calling his shaving oil Sunrise, because the sun rises in Lowestoft, where he lived, as it is the most easterly point of the UK. But one day he was playing cards with his father who turned over the king of spades and suggested he called his oil King of Shaves.

King quickly decided that if his oil was going to be a success it needed to be stocked by Harrods. So using his cold-calling techniques he managed to talk to the owner Mohammed Fayed in person and persuade him to take his oil.

However, making the business a success was hard work. By the end of the first year King had made sales of just £300, with most of the oil sold to friends and family, and had racked up losses of £30,000. When he needed £10,000 to pay for a publicity campaign he had to sell 12.5 per cent of the company to a friend's brother.

He also had to overcome much scepticism. He says: 'We had this tiny little bottle of oil and nobody believed it would work. When I told people I was going to go up against Gillette and change the face of shaving, they would yawn and say: "How are you going to do that?"'

Indeed, people were so convinced he was heading for failure that King started up a sideline business selling surf clothing called Bodyglove, which had featured on the television show *Baywatch*. It was a bad idea. He says: 'It was a nightmare. Everybody thought the clothing business would work really well but none of the surf shops paid their bills and it was hugely time intensive. After two years I closed it down and then I realised I had nearly mucked up King of Shaves because I was juggling too many balls.'

Fortunately, in 1994 he persuaded Boots to stock his oil and by the end of his second year in business sales had risen to £58,000. He says: 'It sat on a Boots shelf with a sad little home-made label stuck on the front of the bottle. But it worked and because it looked quite amateurish people said: "I'll give it a try." I would get phone calls and letters from people saying how it had transformed their life.'

King also worked hard to get editorial coverage in the new wave of men's magazines such as FHM and GQ.

In 1995 he launched a second shaving oil and the following year he launched a range of men's skin care products. By now he had run out of money so he managed to get a £100,000 loan and started invoice discounting to bring in more money.

It was a turning point for the business. King of Shave products began to be stocked in major supermarkets and the company started making fragrances under licence for the clothing chain Ted Baker. A King of Blades razor will be launched in 2006 and King also has plans to expand into the United States.

The business, in which King has a 35 per cent stake, is expected to have sales of close to £15 million in 2006.

Now 40 and separated with one son, King thinks the secret of his success has been to create a product that people actually need. He says: 'You have got to be able to demon-strate that there is a reason for it in people's lives. Why isn't there a five-wheeled car? Because people don't need it.'

It also comes down to a large dose of self-belief. He says: 'You can do anything if you believe you can do it and you have the persistence to actually get on and do it. I enjoy the challenge of doing what people might think is absolutely impossible. People think that Gillette is completely unassail-able sitting at the top of the tree. But big companies were small companies once and people forget that.'

5

Deirdre Bounds
Founder of i to i

Being competitive was something Deirdre Bounds learnt from an early age. The youngest of five children born to an Irish immigrant family on Merseyside, she quickly discovered that nothing came without a struggle. She says: 'We didn't have much and to get anything in the house you really had to figure your way through the household politics – even to keep your portion of dinner from being whipped from your plate when you weren't looking.'

To begin with she had a hard time at school. She says: 'I always looked a bit scruffy and was a bit of an oddball, so at primary school I was the one in the corner with no friends. It was a pretty miserable existence.'

Indeed, Bounds was so unhappy that when she left primary to go to senior school at the age of 11 she was determined things were going to be different. She says: 'I remember deciding that I was going to succeed in everything I did, and that the only person who could change things was me.'

She did well and in 1983 went to Leeds university to study business studies and social science. She initially planned to

be a social worker but a placement at a boys' home convinced her otherwise. So when she graduated she got a job selling advertising space instead.

Then she got a job with a company that made shoe-making machines and was sent to factories around the world to demonstrate the machine. She soon got the travel bug and decided to give up her job. She took a four-week TEFL (teaching English as a foreign language) course and headed for Japan to work as an English teacher there. She ended up staying away for several years, visiting China and Australia and teaching English in Greece.

By the time she returned to the UK, Bound was 30 and still without a clear plan of what to do with her life. So she became a stand-up comedian, performing in Northern clubs. She says: 'I thought I can do anything I want to do and it really doesn't matter what people think of me, I don't care.'

She also became a part-time youth worker and realised that teaching English could be a useful tool for young people taking a gap year before university. She started going into inner city schools to teach TEFL courses.

It was when other people asked if they could take her course that she had her big idea. Bounds decided to quit her job and start up her own company from her bedsit offering weekend TEFL courses, believing that a short course would be more appealing than an expensive four-week course.

She borrowed £1,000 from her parents and put an advert in a local Birmingham paper, thinking that people living there might be more inclined than most to take her course. She says: 'I was driving out of Birmingham one day on a really murky November evening and I thought people really need to leave this city and go somewhere pleasant.' She was right. She got 150 enquiries from the advert. Her first course was attended by 18 people and made her enough money to buy a car.

Inspired by her success, Bounds started holding weekend TEFL courses around the country. They went so well that she soon had to hire a tutor to help her. She says: 'There was no plan or market research, everything I did was based on gut feel because I had no business experience and nobody to ask.'

Fact file

Date of birth: 28 November 1964

Marital status: married with two children

Qualifications: BA (Hons) in business studies and social science from Leeds University

Interests: reading, going to the theatre

Personal philosophy: 'Don't procrastinate. If you have an idea that is sufficiently different and you decide to go for it, take massive action.'

Her unconventional approach did not go down well with everyone, however. 'I think we put quite a few noses out of joint. Somebody at a travel event who ran traditional four-week TEFL courses described us as "that bunch of upstarts from Leeds."'

Undaunted, when people who took her course asked if she could help them find jobs abroad, once again she decided to take up the challenge. She says: 'I wondered if there was any mileage in offering overseas schools some trained volunteer English teachers so my pupils could dip their toe in the water and get two–three months' experience.'

So she sent faxes to several schools overseas and within days got a call from a Russian school that agreed to take some of her teachers. Schools in India and Sri Lanka followed, with each volunteer paying Bounds a fee for organising their stay.

With the business growing fast Bounds moved the office out of her bedsit into a couple of Portakabins at a local college in return for providing some courses. She says: 'I was quite afraid to sign any contracts because I had no idea how the business was going to go.'

But a chance conversation with someone who was advising her on office technology changed her views. She says: 'He told me I had to break out of my frightened shell and move forward.' Inspired by his straight talking, Bounds moved into an office suite and took on more staff. She also started setting up volunteer conservation trips – with the volunteers again paying a fee.

She admits it is an unusual set-up. She says: 'A lot of people pooh-poohed my ideas and said no one would pay to work, but I wanted volunteering abroad to become an exciting travel product and not a dowdy charitable excursion.'

By 1988 there was increasing interest in her volunteer teaching projects from the United States. But people were put off by the need to take a weekend TEFL course in the UK first. So Bounds came up with the unlikely concept of creating an online TEFL course which could be accessed from anywhere in the world. She says: 'When I told people about it they just said, "Don't be ridiculous, you must be joking, nobody is ever going to buy it."'

Undaunted, Bounds went ahead and launched her online course in 1999. Once again, her instincts were spot on. This year 7,000 people will take the online course, making it the main profit earner for the company.

Not everything she had touched has turned to gold. Three years ago, after being frustrated by her lack of Spanish while visiting Honduras she decided to offer weekend Latin-American Spanish courses in Leeds and London. She filled some of the places on the courses but not enough to make it worthwhile and so the idea was shelved.

But i to i now has 300 projects in 24 countries, where people can pay to teach English, work on conservation projects, work in orphanages or build homes. The company, which is expected to have a turnover of £8 million in 2006, has also just launched overland humanitarian tours in Africa and Asia where people do volunteer work en route.

Bounds gets most of her ideas from talking to strangers on trains and planes. She says: 'I am quite inquisitive and often an idea emanates from someone I am talking to. I am quite a fearful flier so generally as the aeroplane is taking off down the runway I will turn to the person sitting next to me and start a conversation. On an eight-hour flight you can tell if someone wants to talk and you can get some great information from people.'

When Bounds finds an idea she likes, she usually acts on instinct. She says: 'Now it might take me a week rather than a couple of minutes. But once I decide on something I do it very quickly, because if it is good it will get copied very quickly.'

One idea she has not yet had time to put into action is a website selling health and fitness holidays. She already has the website name, wellbeingbreaks.com, and even briefly launched the site a couple of Christmases ago. But within three days she realised she did not have the time to commit to making the project work and so pulled the plug on it.

She says: 'I thought there needed to be one portal site for yoga breaks and really good spas. It is still a great idea but I shelved it because I can't focus on too many things at once otherwise nothing gets done effectively. All I am waiting for is the headspace to do it properly. I am learning that I can't do everything.'

She admits that she is driven by the desire to turn ideas into action: 'I like to think up things and I like them to work.'

Now 41 and married with two children, Bounds thinks the secret of her success is to always ask for help. 'There is always somebody else who will know more than I do.'

6

David Sanger
Founder of Rollover Hot Dogs

It took David Sanger several attempts to discover his true calling in life. After leaving university he initially tried his hand at careers in accountancy and advertising. He also considered a career in law and even horticulture before realising that starting up his own business was what he really wanted to do with his life.

Born and brought up in South Africa where his father was an expatriate banker, Sanger moved to England at the age of 10. After boarding school and university he joined a large accountancy firm to train as an accountant but after three years narrowly failed his exams and left without qualifying. He says: 'I hated it. I couldn't stand working with all these notions, concepts and figures. I wanted something more tangible. The whole experience knocked my confidence and led to a lot of soul-searching.'

He enrolled at horticultural college and got a place at law school. But in the end he followed neither direction and took a job with an advertising agency instead. After two years, however, he realised that did not suit him either. He says:

'I got fed up with the endless meetings. The final straw came when six people spent several days trying to decide the background colour for a poster.'

Sanger finally decided the solution was to start his own business. He had no idea what his business would actually do though, so he started looking around for ideas. Initially he thought about opening his own advertising agency. Then became interested in the idea of opening a shoe shop. He says: 'My idea was to sell only the main sizes of shoes, in basic colours, because I read in a book from Harvard Business School that 80 per cent of men have feet sized between 7 and 10. But then I thought actually no, I really don't want to sell shoes.' Eventually he hit upon the idea of opening a chain of sandwich bars so in 2001 at the age of 25 he left his job in advertising.

Using savings of £50,000 and £50,000 borrowed from the bank he opened his first shop in West London and called it Rollover, partly because it was an accounting term and made him laugh. His unique selling point was freshly baked baguettes filled straight from the oven.

But with no experience of the food industry Sanger soon found himself struggling. He was working from 5am to 9pm six days a week but the shop was losing money and after just three months he hit crisis point. He says: 'I was working like a slave, unable to pay myself any salary, with a gloomy future and a 15-year lease. I knew I had to either throw in the towel and go back to being an employee – or find a way of making it work.'

In desperation he decided the answer was to find some wholesale customers. So he hired a manager to run the shop while he went out to secure bulk orders from local hotels and hospitals. Within two months sales had tripled and the business had turned the corner. By 1995 Sanger had managed to grow the business to eight Rollover sandwich bars. But it was clear that they were never going to make him his fortune.

Then one day he was in Copenhagen for the weekend with his Danish girlfriend when he bought a hot dog from a street stall and realised that everyone around him was doing the same. It was at that point he had his big idea. He says: 'They were delicious and I wondered why I would never eat

Fact file

Date of birth: 16 June 1965

Marital status: married with two children

Qualifications: BA (Hons) in economics and politics from Exeter University

Interests: growing bonsai trees, playing squash, swimming, watching rugby

Personal philosophy: 'Live every day as if it is your last.'

one in the UK. I realised it was because at home there was a perception that hot dogs were a poor quality product and something that only children ate. But in Denmark everyone was eating them. So I decided this was the thing for me.'

Even better, unlike those he had eaten in England, these hot dogs were made using a special machine that inserted the sausage right inside the bread roll so that it was completely enclosed, making the hot dog easy to hold and far less messy to eat than conventional ones.

Sanger spent the rest of his weekend in Copenhagen quizzing the street sellers about their hot dogs. He says: 'I drove them all mad asking them questions about how they do it, where they get the hot dogs from, how many they sell.'

By the end of the weekend he had bought a hot dog machine from one of them for £500. When he got it home he asked a British manufacturer to modify the machine so that his customers could see what was going on inside. He says: 'It was a stainless steel box with a spike at one end. All the Danes knew what was inside but I needed to make it understandable for the British consumer who was not used to buying hot dogs. So we changed the stainless steel box to a glass drum so people could see the sausages standing up.'

Then he installed it in one of his sandwich shops, importing high quality sausages from Germany and putting them inside baguettes instead of bread rolls. Soon sales were going so well from that one machine that he asked the manufacturer to make seven more identical ones to put in all his shops.

The name came about by accident. He says: 'We used to wrap our hot dogs in Rollover sandwich bar napkins and customers would come in and ask for a rollover with ketchup. We hadn't intended that to happen but the name stuck.'

One day the landlady of his local pub asked Sanger if she could borrow a machine to make hot dogs for customers watching the rugby international match. He said yes and lent her the machine for the day. She sold out of hot dogs before the match had even started. Two weeks later the pub's area manager called to see if he could hire six machines to install in other pubs and Sanger's wholesale hot dog business was born.

He started selling hot dog machines to pubs and clubs and supplying them with the bread and sausages. It went so well that in 1997 Sanger sold his original sandwich bars for a total of £350,000 to concentrate on growing the hot dog business.

It did not all go according to plan, however. Flushed by the success of his hot dog machines, he decided to open hot dog retail outlets in shopping centres. The first three did well so he went on a high-speed opening spree with £750,000 he borrowed from the bank. He admits: 'I got caught up in it. I opened 18 outlets in 18 months. But it was an absolute disaster. There were staff irregularities and theft and they were losing money. But being an optimist I kept focusing on the good ones instead of the ones that were doing disastrously.'

Fortunately, after 18 months Sanger finally came to his senses and called a halt. Then he spent the next 18 months closing the worst outlets and franchising the rest, losing a great deal of money in the process. He says: 'It was a huge learning curve. I learnt that you have to focus on the whole picture not just on the bit of the picture that you want to see. The failure was not in trying retail, the failure was in doing it too quickly and not stopping and analysing whether it was the right course of action.' Happily, the wholesaling operation remained strong and enabled Rollover to survive its turbulent retail period.

Rollover now sells 25 million hot dogs a year and supplies most premiership football clubs, theme parks and concert halls in the country. It makes eight different varieties of hot dog including chicken and vegetarian and is set to make sales of £10 million in 2006, which will reap more than £2 million in net profit.

Now 40, Sanger still owns 90 per cent of the company and the Danish girlfriend he went to Copenhagen with is now his wife. He still can't quite believe that going on that weekend trip with her provided the inspiration for his success.

He says: 'I am enormously proud of what I've achieved. It has definitely been worth it. It is not making money that has inspired me, it is wanting to be the biggest and best.'

He thinks that finding a good business idea is just a matter of keeping your eyes open. He says: 'Very few of us wake up and invent a mobile phone or a new car engine. Most of us just tweak something that has been around and improve it. Entrepreneurs aren't generally born with a vocation, they tend to look at lots of ideas and jump on the train of opportunity as it races past.'

7

Anthony Ward Thomas
Founder of Ward Thomas
Removals

Anthony Ward Thomas was working as a salesman for an aluminium company when a chance conversation with his boss changed his life. Ward Thomas says: 'My boss told me that by the age of 27 I really should know what I was doing with my life because it would be the last chance to make something of myself.'

It was just the wake-up call he needed. The words of advice stayed with him and a few months before he turned 27 Ward Thomas looked around at the aluminium firm and realised that it was not somewhere he wanted to spend the rest of his life.

So, to force himself to take action, he quit his job and gave himself two months to work out where his future lay. He says: 'If I hadn't left my job I would have turned up for work every day like anybody else. Leaving gave me the incentive to actually do something.'

Born in London and brought up in Essex, Ward Thomas was one of six children. His father was a businessman and

his mother was a successful novelist and he was sent away to boarding school at the age of seven. He says: 'As a child I was quite shy to begin with, but at boarding school you tend to develop a fairly tough outer shell and so I became quite gregarious.'

He left school at 18 to join the army but after three months was asked to leave. Over the next few years he took a number of casual jobs including fork-lift truck driver and double glazing salesman.

When Ward Thomas quit his job to make something of himself all he knew was that he wanted to set up his own business. His first idea was to start up a business that did people's supermarket shopping for them. He says: 'I was going to get orders from, say, 500 people for their weekly shop. I would have a van and would do the shopping and deliver it and put it away in their cupboards.' He had a meeting with a supermarket to discuss how much discount he could get if he used them exclusively. Then he started looking into the logistics of how the service would actually work. He says: 'I went quite a way down the line with it and it was all quite do-able. It was quite exciting.'

But then he had a meeting with a stockbroker and in their research department he discovered that many people, rather than finding their supermarket shopping a big chore, actually saw it as the highlight of their week. He says: 'I discovered that people like to get out and see what is new on the shelves and compare the prices.'

In hindsight he says it is perhaps just as well he abandoned his plans. Soon afterwards the internet arrived and the supermarkets themselves started offering delivery services.

Ward Thomas then started researching two other types of business he quite liked the look of – the furniture removal business and the funeral business. He explains: 'I just looked at the simplest things. I thought that it didn't take an academic mind to be able to dig a hole and stick someone in it, and it certainly didn't take an academic mind to go into someone's house and take a piece of furniture and put it in a lorry and deliver it somewhere else.'

He had a meeting with Howard Hodgson, who had revolutionised the funeral industry in the 1980s by buying up family-run businesses and revamping the services they

Fact file

Date of birth: 19 March 1958

Marital status: married with three children

Qualifications: three A levels

Interests: riding horses

Personal philosophy: 'If you make a decision, stick by it even if it is wrong. If you keep changing your mind you would never get out of bed.'

offered, after bumping into him by chance in the waiting room of a doctors' surgery. Ward Thomas says: 'I would love to have turned the idea of a funeral on its head a bit.' But the idea of setting up a funeral business was decisively quashed by his wife, who said she couldn't think of anything worse than dealing with dead bodies all the time.

So Ward Thomas went to work for a furniture removal company for a few weeks to find out how the industry worked. He was horrified by what he discovered. He says: 'I learnt all there was to learn about how not to be a removal man – how to steal, how to be dishonest. It was dreadful. I couldn't believe what I was seeing. Four furniture removal men would go into a house and all four of them would steal – money, drink, clothes, whatever wouldn't be noticed until weeks later.'

It was then that he had his big idea. He realised that the problem with traditional removals firms was the type of people working for them. So he decided to set up a removals company of his own and employ only young men aged between 19 and 24, many of whom had come to the UK from Australia and New Zealand in search of work, whom he thought would be fitter and more honest than the older workers traditionally employed by removal firms.

He bought a second-hand removal lorry for £5,000 at auction, paying a £1,000 deposit for it, which was all the money he had. Then he persuaded the bank to lend him the rest. He says: 'I phoned my bank manager up and said if you don't lend me the money I am going to lose £1,000. So they lent me the money.'

His first commission came via his wife, who told colleagues at the publishing company where she worked about his new business. He says: 'I earned more in that one day than I did in a month as a salesman selling aluminium.'

It was slow going. It took Ward Thomas three months to get his second job. But by the end of the first year the business was doing well enough for him to buy a second lorry and after two years he bought a third.

He explains: 'The young men I employed were pleasant to be with and the customers loved them – moving is such a ghastly experience that if you can dilute the ghastliness a bit you are a hero.'

But then recession hit. Ward Thomas says: 'There was nothing I could do. I couldn't force people to buy and sell their houses, I couldn't force people to move, I couldn't discount things. I was staring at a blank diary.'

Ward Thomas survived the downturn largely thanks to the Carlton Towers Hotel which employed him to move the contents of the entire hotel, and a lady client who had six houses.

As the housing market recovered so did his business and Ward Thomas started adding new lorries. He had a fear of borrowing money to expand the business so each time he bought lorries he paid for them outright with cash from company funds.

His caution has paid off. He now has 42 lorries and the company has a turnover of £8 million.

Two years ago he heard that another furniture removal company, Moves, was close to receivership and so bought it for £200,000 from company funds. He also sold 15 per cent of the company to his management to encourage them to stay with the company and retains the remaining 85 per cent himself.

For Ward Thomas the secret of a successful business idea is to take an existing idea and then do it slightly differently. He says: 'The biggest mistake people make when they embark on an entrepreneurial type of career is they try to reinvent the wheel. New ideas are dangerous because they just never seem to work. A great example of something which is not a new idea is Prêt a Manger. All they are is sandwiches, but the secret of their success is consistency and freshness. And that's really all Ward Thomas Removals is – it is a simple business done with a slightly different angle.'

In his case that has meant deliberately staffing his removals firm with a very different type of workforce than traditional firms used. He says: 'In this business you are only as good as the guy who is lifting the sofa. That really is what it boils down to. I can go into to someone's house and promise the earth but if Jo Gorilla turns up it is a problem.'

Ward Thomas is now aged 48, with a wife and three children. He has used some of the money he has earned to buy a couple of race horses which he rides himself in point to point meetings.

He says: 'I am enormously proud of the business because we have been competing in a world where there are some very good businesses and an awful lot of rubbish. You have got to be very convincing to charge the sort of prices that we charge and yet still get the business.'

8

Lara Morgan
Founder of Pacific Direct

Five years ago Lara Morgan promised her staff that if the firm's profits ever reached £1 million, she would take them all on holiday to Barbados. Last year she delivered on her promise. Morgan and her 26 staff flew to the Caribbean for an all-expenses paid week-long holiday.

It is not the first time Lara has showed her appreciation to her staff. Last year she sent them all a huge bouquet of flowers after they exceeded their monthly sales figures. Another time she taped £50 notes to the bottom of their chairs for them to find.

She says: 'It is just a laugh. There are a lot more good people in this world than there are bad, and if you give people a chance then it generally produces motivation, teamwork and momentum. It is very important to me that we have fun in the workplace. I am here so many hours of the day that if I am not enjoying it, then what's the point?'

Born in Germany, where her father was serving as an officer in the British army, Morgan was brought up in Hong Kong after her father was relocated there and from the age of

11 was sent to boarding school in Scotland. She left school at 18 to get a job in Hong Kong selling business gifts to banks and airlines.

After three years she went to live in the Middle East with her fiancé where she sold advertising space for *Yellow Pages*, ending up as national accounts manager overseeing 128 people. She admits: 'I was in completely over my head, it was sink or swim. But I like having a challenge.'

When the Gulf war started in 1991 Morgan and her fiancé moved to New Zealand where she ran triathlons instead of working until the two of them returned to the UK so that her fiancé could study for an MBA. On the way home they stopped off in Hong Kong to see her parents where Morgan was approached by the company she had worked for selling business gifts and asked if she wanted to try selling them in the UK.

She said yes and her big idea was born. On arrival in the UK started ringing round hotels. She got her first order, for a pre-threaded needle sewing kit, from the Dorchester Hotel in London. She says: 'As I left their office they reminded me that they would only take a few at a time, invoiced as and when delivered, delivered within 24 hours, and I was expected to hold stock, did I have a warehouse and would the items be customised – to which I said yes that was all fine. Which was utter rubbish – the warehouse was underneath my fax machine at home.'

She discovered she had a talent for selling, however, and by the end of her first year as a one-man band had managed to rack up sales of £108,000, having imported all the products from Asia. She says: 'I used to get up at six and drive to London, do five or six appointments and be back in the office by about four in the afternoon. Then I used to do everything else – the rubbish bins, the phone, the fax, quotes, typing, the accounts, all my bookkeeping.'

It was largely a process of trial and error. She says: 'I was continually asking people what to do. It is of huge value if you have no pride and no shame and are willing to say: "Look I don't know what I am doing, could you help?" There was no planning involved.'

As sales mounted the business outgrew her relationship with her fiancé and she moved to live in a one-bedroom flat which doubled as an office. Indeed, she continued to work

Fact file

Date of birth: 16 December 1967

Marital status: married with three children

Qualifications: three A levels

Interests: reading business books, playing sports, going to the theatre and musicals

Personal philosophy: 'If you don't ask, you don't get.'

from home for the next four years until her new boyfriend insisted that the office move elsewhere.

Then in 1996 European cosmetic regulations changed, making importing products more difficult and she decided it was time her company started making its own products. She spent £200,000 opening a factory in China and another £39,000 taking over one in the Czech Republic. She says: 'We did them at the same time, rather stupidly. It was not planned. I bought the factory in China and then our Czech supplier said they'd run out of cash and could I find some. I said: "Yes – in return for 51 per cent of your company."'

The gamble paid off and the business continued to grow, helped by Morgan's enthusiasm for encouraging her staff to stay focused on the business. She took business books with her to read whenever she had to travel abroad for work and each time came back brimming with new ideas. She says: 'My first three employees used to shake in their boots because I would come back from a trip with two or three books where I had turned over the corner of the pages and scribbled all over them. The first thing I would do after trips was photocopy pages of these books and put them in their in-trays with a note saying: "You might be interested in this, do have a look at this, read this."'

She also discovered two books by an author called Bob Nelson which struck a chord. One was called *1001 Ways to Energise Employees*, and the other one *1001 Ways to Reward Employees*. She says: 'I have got a business library in the office and whenever one of my employees does a good job I go down there and read a page. What is really exciting is that I turn over the top right hand corner if it is a good idea but I turn over the bottom corner if it is a great idea. So I even have a structure. If I really like a book I have got two copies of it.'

She admits: 'My staff take the piss out of me relentlessly. Some of the titles are so naff and yet there is something that attracts me to them. I think a lot of entrepreneurs constantly strive to improve their businesses but I just look for the simplest, fastest ways.'

By 1999 the business was growing so fast that Morgan realised it was time to work out where it was actually heading. So she booked herself onto a four-month business growth development course at Cranfield Business School in order to write a business plan. While she was there she also came up with the idea of incentivising her staff with the promise of a free holiday to Barbados.

She says: 'When I wrote my business plan I decided to come up with something which meant that not only was I demanding a huge amount, I was also going to reward it with a similar amount. When you are making profits of £200,000 it seems pretty arrogant to say we are going to make £1 million profit and so I felt it was a good idea to give people a significant return.'

Before her incentive could become reality however the business hit a major hurdle. Two years ago, with the tourism industry on its knees, Morgan was forced to make 30 per cent of her staff redundant.

She says: 'I almost lost everything. The combination of the buildings coming down in America, foot and mouth, Sars, chicken flu, the run up to the Iraq war and then general devastation of global travel meant that we weren't seeing the same growth. It was pretty serious.'

She survived by staying determinedly upmarket and selling to only the best hotels. Pacific Direct is now expected to make around £2.5 million profit in 2006 on sales of around £17.5 million. It supplies hotels in 103 countries including the Waldorf Astoria in New York, and Sandy Lane in Barbados.

Now 38, with three children, and a husband Charlie who runs the company's IT department, she thinks the secret of her success is to be continually learning. She says: 'I read business books passionately like a lunatic whenever I travel. I have just come back from a trip to Italy and on the way I read business magazines and when I came back I put 18 different sheets of photocopied articles into people's trays which had been scribbled on and circled. There was an article on rent negotiation, there was one on new technology so I put that in the IT guy's tray, and there was a marketing one on websites. I invest in my staff a lot – but I haven't forgotten myself because I also need to learn a lot.' Morgan is also a great believer in doing things her way. She says: 'I like to do things differently. I don't want to be anyone but me.'

9

Paul Stanyer

Founder of HolidayTaxis.com

When Paul Stanyer passed O levels in 10 subjects, he became so confident of his ability to do well at A levels that he decided to take five of them. He ended up passing just one – in art. He says: 'I just took on too much. I thought I could breeze through them but I overextended myself.'

It was not an ideal situation to be in. One of five children, Stanyer lived in the northern industrial town of Consett where thanks to the closure of the steelworks there was 40 per cent unemployment.

His father, who worked for British Telecom, decided that Stanyer should take an accountancy foundation course at the local polytechnic. But before the course started Stanyer went to stay with his sister in Spain who was working there as a rep for a holiday company. He says: 'I saw how much fun she was having and I thought, hold on a minute. I could spend four years in a classroom or could I get into this lifestyle.' So he abandoned the polytechnic place, enrolled on a Spanish course and the following summer got a job on a caravan park in Spain.

He hated it. He says: 'I was so lonely. It was three weeks before I saw another English person. The other thing I hadn't taken into account was having to clean all these caravans after every departure. My mother had struggled to get me to clean my bedroom for 20 years so it was all a bit much.'

Luckily his sister came to the rescue again, and told him that a holiday company in Greece was looking for reps. Within a few weeks Stanyer was in Corfu. This time he loved it. 'I was in a Mediterranean resort where every night was Saturday night, they gave me a brand new apartment to live in and a motorbike – and they were paying me. It was fabulous.'

Stanyer spent the following two summers working in Corfu but when a holidaymaker at the resort died after drinking too much he decided it was time for a change. He says: 'He was 21, the same age as me at the time. I just thought enough is enough.'

So he returned to the UK and got a job as an area sales manager for the same company. By the time he was 24 he had been promoted to national sales manager. He soon realised though that the corporate world was not for him. He says: 'I was earning good money and had a company car but I was fed up with driving round the M25 and I thought there was more to life than having strategy meetings and going to conferences. I decided I was too young to be in this position at this stage in my life and that there was a lot more fun to be had.'

Within a few months the decision of whether to leave his job was taken for him when the company merged with another firm and he was made redundant. He spent the next 10 months playing golf and wondering what to do next. Then he headed back to Greece to be a manager for another holiday company and ended up staying eight years, working his way up the company.

At the age of 34, however, he was made redundant for a second time. He says: 'I was totally stunned. It really was a case of what do I do now?' He came back to the UK but struggled to get a job. He says: 'It was incredible how much my life overseas was devalued. I was regional manager for large holiday companies with multi-million pound budgets

Fact file

Date of birth: 17 November 1965

Marital status: partnered with one child

Qualifications: one A level

Interests: playing golf, watching rugby, football and cricket

Personal philosophy: 'You die if you worry, you die if you don't, so why worry about anything?'

– and I got back and people thought I had been a holiday rep.'

He decided it might be better to start up a business of his own. He says: 'I decided that I didn't want to be working until I was 65 and then be given a carriage clock. And I didn't want to be stuck in an office answering to some idiot who I didn't even like. I wanted a bit more choice in my life.'

He initially toyed with the idea of doing something that involved golf. He says: 'Golf is one of my passions in life but after a few months of researching the market I decided that there was just way too much competition.'

It was while having a few drinks in the pub with a couple of former colleagues that he came up with his big idea. The three of them started talking about how tour operators had recently started charging people to use their transfer buses to take them from the airport to their hotels. Stanyer decided he could offer a better, faster service by providing taxis to take people to their holiday resorts instead. He says: 'I thought it was outrageous for tour operators to charge for transfers because it meant that it was not a package holiday any more.'

Both his former colleagues thought it was a great idea too and over the next few days Stanyer, with the help of one of his colleagues, registered several possible website addresses for the company including HolidayTaxis.com.

He then did absolutely nothing at all about his idea. It was six months later, when he was doing some consultancy work for a fledgling hotel company, when he suddenly realised that his transfer service idea could have bigger potential than he had initially thought. He realised that his taxi transfers could appeal to the growing number of independent travellers as well.

He says: 'When I saw the way the market was heading I had a major rethink of the whole thing. It became apparent to me that there were two market sectors to attack – there were those people who were dissatisfied with coach transfers and those people who were travelling independently. I thought if I don't do this, and quickly, then somebody else will figure this out and do it.'

Others, however, were not convinced it was a good idea. When Stanyer presented his business plan to a travel company which he thought might be interested in becoming an investor, he got short shrift. He says: 'I had an investment meeting with the only person who was willing to talk to me and I was actually laughed out of the office. He told me it was never going to make any money, that I was wasting my time and should do something else.'

Eventually, one of his former colleagues who liked the idea put Stanyer in touch with some Indonesian investors who agreed to put in £100,000 in return for a 50 per cent stake in the company. Then Stanyer found a technology company to build the website and gave them a stake instead of paying them, leaving him with 20 per cent. He says: 'I didn't have any money myself so it was a case of having 100 per cent of nothing or 20 per cent of something that was now a project.'

He launched the website in March 2003 and by May a thousand travel agents had registered. But in June Stanyer hit a problem. He says: 'I had totally underestimated the demand for vehicle sizes other than taxis. Our website would only allow people to book a taxi so we had to take the bookings for other vehicles over the telephone. We were in danger of becoming a call centre – which defeated the objective of being a technology-based solution.'

After much agonising Stanyer decided that rather than bolt on new technology to his existing website, it would be more sensible to rebuild it entirely. As a result he was not able to promote the company until it was fully functioning.

He has since made up for lost time. In 2006 HolidayTaxis.com is expected to have sales of £7.5 million and currently operates in 30 countries. Stanyer has also launched two related companies – BusinessTaxis.com, which provides corporate transfers, and Destination Care, an in-resort representation service for independent travellers.

He also has one other idea which he hopes to start turning into a reality soon. He says: 'I am a great observer in life. I see things and think about how they could be improved. I just can't help myself.'

Now 40 with a son, he says: 'What motivates me is that I want to be the master of my own destiny. I don't want to spend three hours a day in my car driving round the M25. And I don't want to rely on working for someone else to make me rich or happy. I want to have control of my life.'

10

Robert Hughes
Founder of Wesco

At the age of 28 Robert Hughes was living in California working for the commercial arm of a US bank. He was not happy. He says: 'I hated my job. I was completely bored and became a clock watcher. And I realised that there was a very good chance I was going to be equally bored in another job so I had better do something different.'

Brought up in Cheshire, Hughes always dreamt of setting up his own business and after leaving school took a business degree at Thames Polytechnic, now the University of Greenwich. He says: 'My father was a self-employed insurance broker and my mother's family all had their own businesses. The culture at home was very much that, if you were going to make it in this life, you had to do it on your own.'

But unsure of how to realise his ambition, Hughes initially took a job with a leasing company. After seven years in the corporate world however, he realised that if he really wanted to follow his dream then it was now or never.

He decided that he wanted to start up an export business selling unusual US products back home in England. When

he had been at polytechnic a former graduate had returned to tell the class how he had set himself up in business as the UK import and distribution agent for a German company that made garden machinery. Hughes says: 'I thought it was the perfect job because you got to use languages and there was foreign travel involved – but you were your own boss.'

Hughes did some research and found a couple of unusual products he liked in California, but he was not convinced that people would want to buy them in the UK. The first was a cover for automobiles called a nose bra which strapped across the bonnet to protect the car from stone chips. The second was a windscreen visor which fitted behind the windscreen to keep the car cool. He says: 'Both those ideas appealed very much, but they were both very southern California and didn't wear so well in wet climates.'

Then one day he was at a friend's house for coffee when another friend Hughes had never met happened to pop in.

They started chatting and during their conversation Hughes heard about something which was to become his big idea.

The visitor was a joiner and mentioned that he was doing some work at the home of a lawyer who had invented an alarm clock that was made like a baseball. When the alarm went off in the morning, you threw the ball at the wall to switch it off.

Hughes was transfixed. He says: 'It was like the scales had been lifted from my eyes. I thought it sounded like a fantastic product that I could sell in England. Everybody hates getting up in the morning and the idea of taking out your early morning anger on your clock just seemed the perfect idea.'

The next day Hughes phoned the lawyer and asked to meet him. Over lunch the lawyer agreed to give Hughes exclusive rights to sell the baseball alarm clock in Britain, provided he was prepared to buy 30,000 of them upfront. Hughes did not have the money to do that but fortunately his father had recently retired after selling his own insurance business and agreed to act as guarantor at the bank. So Hughes was able to borrow the money he needed to buy the clocks. Then he asked his father and an old school friend to help him sell the alarm clock to mail order companies in Britain.

It quickly became clear that there was big demand for the baseball clock, and so Hughes decided to branch out into

Fact file

Date of birth: 10 April 1968

Marital status: married with two children

Qualifications: BA (Hons) in international marketing from Thames Polytechnic

Interests: boating, golf, watching football

Personal philosophy: 'Don't fail.'

other items. He managed to find another dozen unusual products from California which he thought he might be able to sell in Britain, including a Garfield wristwatch.

Sales went so well that after six months he gave up his job with the bank in California and returned to England to set up his own company, which he called Wesco. Then he started running the business full time from the basement of his father's house.

With sales of his imported products going well, Hughes started acquiring licences to make products based on film and television characters. He decided to start with a Bart Simpson clock that spoke in the character's voice when the alarm went off. He says: 'Nobody had ever done that before and it was a phenomenal success. We sold about 250,000 of those clocks.'

He took on more licences and the business grew to include watches, radios and money boxes, with the company designing all the products in Britain and getting them made in Chinese factories. Each time Hughes followed the guiding principle that every product he sold had to have a purpose. He says: 'I decided that whatever I imported had to have a purpose as well as being fun. Because if a product has absolutely no function then within two months it will end up in the back of a cupboard somewhere because the novelty had worn off. But even once the novelty of throwing your alarm clock at the wall has worn off, it still tells the time and it will still wake you up in the morning.'

Six years ago, however, the business was suddenly plunged into crisis. The US dollar fell sharply in value and Wesco was hit by currency losses of £180,000. At the same time, two of the licences it had bought, for the movie *Chicken Run* and the television series *The Royle Family*, turned out to be duds, losing the company £250,000 over two years.

Hughes says: 'We had been making money hand over fist with the animated characters Wallace and Gromit, so when we were offered *Chicken Run*, which was another Nick Park production, we thought it couldn't fail. But the reason

Wallace and Gromit did well is that Gromit is a cute little dog. Chickens aren't cute. Why would you want to cuddle a chicken? You would get your eyes pecked out.'

By the start of 2002, after two years of losses, Hughes realised that he had two stark choices: sell the business or turn it around and make it profitable again. He says: 'It was a pivotal moment. I talked about selling it with my wife every day.'

When someone offered him a paltry amount to take the business off his hands, however, Hughes realised he was not about to give up that easily. 'The money on offer was pitiful compared with what the business was really worth,' he says. 'I decided that I had made the business work for 13 of the previous 15 years, so I could do it again.'

Hughes reduced his workforce by two people, recruited in-house designers and hired a new sales team. Then he decided to expand the product range into lifestyle gifts.

He immediately struck gold with a Simpsons talking bottle opener, selling more than 600,000 of them. Then he did the same with a girls' accessory range called Groovy Chick, which became a huge success.

The firm now sells a range of 250 products compared with 50 five years ago and has annual sales of £7 million, most of them to Argos, Boots and Debenhams.

Hughes says that dealing with the crisis was a big learning curve: 'After 13 years of making profits there was a feeling that we couldn't make products fast enough and that it was easy. But the experience of those two years re-instilled in me the fear of failure.'

He admits to being very cautious in his business dealings, something he thinks he learnt from his time working in a bank. He says: 'I worry more about telling a best friend that I have just gone bankrupt than I would about telling a complete stranger that I have just made another million. That is the driver for me. If I can stay in business until I am 55, I will be a happy boy.'

Now 38, Hughes says he had always felt the need to carve out his own destiny. 'I have to have my own way,' he says. 'If I don't get my own way, I am not happy. I sometimes have to stop myself because I go home and am still playing the managing director.'

He says that one of his primary motivations has been his father. 'My sister became a lawyer and then a judge and was the apple of my dad's eye,' he says. 'So one of my biggest driving forces was the desire for my father's approval, because she had it in spades. Now when he talks about his children I know that I get as much airtime as my sister.'

11

Hilary Andrews
Founder of Mankind

Hilary Andrews' love affair with cosmetics began early on in life. She says: 'A friend of my grandmother's worked in a factory where they made Mary Quant and Miners cosmetics. Every now and then she would give me a bag of them and it was the most amazing thing anyone could ever have given me. I used to play with them for hours.'

Born in Woking, Surrey, Andrews grew up surrounded by a family where everyone worked for themselves, her father running a building and landscaping company and her sister running her own public relations agency. She went to sixth form college to do A levels but left halfway through the course to train as a beauty therapist at a private college.

She says: 'My typing teacher asked me if I was ever going to work in an office. When I said no she said I should decide what I wanted to do and go and do it. I had no doubt in my mind that I wanted to be a make-up artist or work in the beauty industry.'

On leaving college Andrews worked in a beauty salon for four years in Chobham and then in 1983, at the age of 23,

opened a salon on her own in Woking. It went well but after seven years she decided that it was time for a new challenge. So she took a teacher training course, and then a degree in education, and taught beauty and holistic therapy in a college in Farnborough, Surrey.

She toyed with the idea of doing a second degree in education but realised that she really missed working in the beauty industry. So she got a job as a training manager with a company that distributed products to the spa industry. As part of her job Andrews trained some of the staff who were going to work at a new men's spa in London called The Refinery. It got her thinking.

She says: 'We adapted a lot of the treatments to suit men and it really sparked my interest. There was a lot of buzz in the industry about the male grooming market and how it was really going to take off.'

Excited by the potential of this new market she moved to the mail order department of the distribution company she worked for in order to gain more experience of selling. She says: 'You can only go so far with training and I decided I wanted to do something a bit more dynamic within the company. I find retail and selling very exciting and I felt this was a big opportunity.'

Within six months of being there, however, Andrews had decided that if she was going to make the most of the opportunity of the emerging male grooming market then she had to do it on her own. She says: 'I was being asked by men what I could recommend for them to use on their skin and realised there was obviously a real market for this.'

So in 2000 she took the plunge and left her job to start up her own company selling men's beauty products by mail order. She says: 'It was scary but I thought I am 39 and if I don't do it now then I am never going to do it. I wanted to prove that I could make something a real success.'

She began by finding a business partner, Paul Jameson, who had been running an electronics company. She says: 'He was introduced to me by a mutual friend. We didn't really know each other but we had a chat about it and both got really fired up about it. He seemed to balance out my skills.'

Fact file

Date of birth: 16 October 1961

Marital status: married with one child

Qualifications: BA (Hons) in post-compulsory education from Union Saint Éclair college

Interests: writing children's books, gardening, going to the theatre

Personal philosophy: 'Look after people on the way up because you never know when you might meet them on the way down.'

They tried to get finance from private investors but found that no one was prepared to invest in such an untried area. 'The dot com boom had ended and every one was panicking because the bubble had bust. People were saying they weren't going to invest in male grooming because it was such as unknown area and they didn't really believe that men would buy that kind of thing.'

Eventually, the two of them they managed to raise £50,000 from their own resources, with Andrews putting in £10,000 which she raised from remortgaging her house and Jameson putting in £20,000. They borrowed the rest from two family members and two friends who came up with £5,000 each. Meanwhile, Andrews got a part-time evening job teaching at a beauty college for the first year while her husband paid their mortgage.

Then Andrews and Jameson bought some mailing lists and got 100,000 catalogues printed which friends and family helped them pack into envelopes and mail out. They got enough of a response from the mail-out to give them an initial customer base and quickly realised that men much preferred ordering over the internet than by mail order. It was a discovery that would transform the business.

She says: 'We knew that were guys out there who wanted to use these products but they just weren't accessible. They didn't want the hassle of going to a shop and speaking to a consultant. The internet has made it very easy to buy products that were previously difficult to buy and enabled us to give people a lot of information about them. We believe that if we educate people in the benefits of these products they will try them. Ninety-nine per cent of our sales are through the internet now.'

As the business took off Andrews and Jameson hired some staff and moved the office to Farnham, where they have also opened a spa next door. She says: 'We have watched things develop very quickly in both the male grooming and the internet market. But we have tried to control the growth so we don't run before we can walk.'

Mankind's turnover is expected to be £4 million in 2006. It recently opened a dedicated male grooming area in Harvey Nichols stores in Manchester and Dublin.

Now 44 and married with a young son, Andrews thinks the secret of her success has been to keep her emotional attachment to the business separate from the need to take practical decisions. She says: 'I think it is really important for anyone who is going to start a new business to separate out the emotional side from the practical side. A lot of people get so excited about an idea that they don't really look at the figures and see how the concept can work. You have to have faith in your idea but you also have to stand back from it emotionally instead of just saying this is what I have always wanted to do. I think it is a mistake to let the emotion overtake you.'

That has meant being very focused on how the business operates. She says: 'You have to watch the bottom line constantly. It is not about starting a business and getting yourself a nice car, it is about starting a business and having a really solid model that works.'

Andrews has also been very careful to limit her risk to what she could cope with if it all went wrong. She says: 'I am quite a cautious person and I always think about what is the worst possible thing that can happen. If I can live with that then I go for it. If I wanted to do something which meant I couldn't survive if something went wrong, then I wouldn't do it. Some people would, but I wouldn't.'

Despite her cautious approach, Andrews is constantly having other ideas for potential businesses. She says: 'I am very interested in the teenage grooming market because I think it is another big growth area.' Indeed, she once toyed with the idea of opening a make-up shop but the high cost of renting premises deterred her.

Her next big idea is to do something involving chocolate. She says: 'I am very interested in the food industry and I am particularly interested in chocolate. I think the trends in this country are very much about people being cosy and wanting comfort food and comfort eating.'

For now, however, Mankind remains the focus of her attention. She says: 'What motivates me is being successful in an industry that I love. To have the respect of my peers is tremendous. It gives me such a kick. And I love the way that cosmetics can transform people. It is the most rewarding thing to give people confidence.'

12

David Salisbury

Founder of David Salisbury Conservatories

David Salisbury took the long way round to becoming an entrepreneur.

At the age of 21 he was all set for an academic career in the outer limits of theoretical physics. He says: 'I wanted to be at the forefront of studying the building blocks of the universe.'

Salisbury was born in South London. His father worked in the accounts department for the Corporation of London and his mother was a housewife. After leaving school Salisbury went to Oxford University and then embarked on a PhD doctorate at Sussex University. But two and a half years into the three-year course Salisbury suddenly realised he was heading in the wrong direction. He says: 'I realised that although I had done quite well, I wasn't going to be as successful as I had hoped. I was unlikely to be the next Einstein. So I lost interest.'

He decided to become a deep-sea diver instead and after a six-week course got a job diving for oil in the North Sea and

then in the Persian Gulf. He says: 'My parents were definitely worried.'

After three years of diving, however, at the age of 27
Salisbury realised that although he enjoyed it, this was not a
job he could do forever. He initially toyed with the idea of
buying a boat and sailing around the world in it, but he was
also becoming increasingly interested in the idea of
psychotherapy, spirituality and mental health. So he
returned to the UK and worked as a volunteer with home-
less people. After a year out travelling with his girlfriend he
got a job in a hostel for people with mental problems.

He says: 'Having failed to get to the bottom of what made
everything tick by doing physics I decided wanted to get to
the bottom of it through the mind. I used to sit up into the
night talking to people about their problems.'

At the same time Salisbury started up a small carpentry
workshop at the hostel as a form of occupational therapy
for the patients. Gradually he realised that carpentry was

something he enjoyed doing too. He says: 'I started getting quite obsessed with the idea of making things to a high standard.'

Making things with his hands was in many ways a return to the pursuits he had enjoyed as a child. While growing up, Salisbury used to enjoy spending much of his time on his own taking apart and building objects. He says: 'I was given a pre-war radio by a relative which I took to pieces. And I liked making things but I had unrealistic ideas about what I could make. When I was seven I saw a picture of a flying machine in a comic and I tried to make one out of bits of wood.'

In his spare time Salisbury began helping out a friend who made furniture for a living and when his interest in mental health started to wane he decided he wanted to start up his own business making furniture. He persuaded his wife to move out of London and in 1982 they moved to a house in Somerset which had a workshop in the garden where Salisbury, now 32, could make his furniture.

He made a couple of pieces and while setting up his workshop he accidentally discovered another source of revenue. He says: 'I wanted a really nice cabinet maker's work bench to work on so I decided that, rather than buy one, I would make one out of solid beech. It took three or four weeks to make and was absolutely beautiful. But having made it there

Fact file

Date of birth: 9 April 1950

Marital status: married with two children

Qualifications: BA (Hons) in physics from Oxford University

Interests: photography, walking, travelling

Personal philosophy: 'One day at a time.'

were certain dissatisfactions I had about it and I thought I could have done it better. But the only way I could justify the idea to myself of making another one was to think in terms of selling them.' So Salisbury started selling his solid beech work benches and took orders for 150 of them.

However, he soon realised that making furniture and work benches would not provide a decent living for his family in the long term. So he switched to doing restoration joinery work, supplying pieces to a local tradesman.

One day the tradesman was asked to build a conservatory and asked Salisbury to help. It was a revelatory experience. He says: 'I was hooked by the way the roof went together. We had to order double glazed units of different shapes so using my physics background I got out my pen and worked out all the angles and glass sizes. So that when we took the conservatory out to site it just fitted together.'

It was a novel approach in an industry where most wooden conservatories were made on a trial and error basis by cutting and trying the different pieces over and over again until they fitted together. It was then that Salisbury had his big idea. Excited by the discovery that his knowledge of maths and physics could enable him to do things more efficiently, Salisbury started to design and build conservatories by himself, writing computer programs to calculate every dimension to make sure that the pieces fitted perfectly together.

He says: 'I wanted to pre-calculate everything. I wanted to calculate what all the cuts had to be and what all the glass sizes were so that when I arrived on site that would be the first time the conservatory had been put together. One advantage for me of doing this was that I simply didn't have the space to build a conservatory in the small workshop I had.'

Salisbury started selling more conservatories and in 1989 moved the business to a unit on an industrial estate. He also bought his first suit. About this purchase he says: 'Looking back, I don't know whether it was really necessary – or whether it was just because I thought that I needed to look like a businessman so that people would take me seriously.'

But as the business overheads grew he found it hard to make a profit. He says: 'It was really difficult because we didn't have the critical mass and turnover to support the infrastructure. I was still doing everything – all the selling, all the accounts, all the management functions – but when I tried to delegate some of it I found that unless I spent time in the factory then we would lose money. There were always so many things half done. I could never come home on a Friday night and think that every problem was put to bed.'

In 1995, however, the business finally grew to the point where it could make the transition from cottage industry to proper business. Salisbury brought in two minority shareholders who each took 10 per cent of the company and made one of them a director.

The company now has 112 employees and in 2006 is expected to have sales of £9.2 million. Its conservatories sell for an average price of £35,000–40,000 and go up to £200,000. Five years ago the company moved into its own purpose-built factory which has since doubled in size.

Salisbury has also increasingly applied his love of computer technology to organise the way the entire company runs. He says: 'I think one of the reasons I have been successful is because I have got passionately into IT. The whole company is run on IT structures that I have built – the account systems are integrated into means of measurement and into means of looking at costs, for example. All the databases use home-grown IT and so do all the processes involved in manufacturing and calculating sizes. We make our conservatory roofs now on a sophisticated computer-controlled machine which automatically cuts all the angles and does all the moulds, and I am looking at a new generation of that which would be even more efficient because it would automatically load the timber and read the bar code.'

Now 56, Salisbury still does not regard himself as a natural entrepreneur. He says: 'Business is what I had to do in order to indulge my obsessions and to pursue particular ideas. I wanted to pursue the idea of how I could do something better.'

Indeed, he thinks the secret of his success has been his obsessive nature. 'That is certainly what my wife would say and I think it is true. It is about having a kind of perfectionism and wanting to get things right. I really dislike things being half done or not finished. That is what keeps driving me forward because I always want to get to that point.'

13

Karl Massey
Founder of Cottrills

For many entrepreneurs starting out, the biggest difficulty is finding sales. Karl Massey, however, faced quite the opposite problem.

Massey was brought up in Macclesfield, Cheshire, and at the age of 13 began working for his father on Saturdays at a small jewellery shop in Alderley Edge which specialised in second-hand and antique jewellery. When he left school two years later he went to work there full time. He says: 'I absolutely loved it.'

Between 1980 and 1985 the family business expanded to include four jewellery shops, but when Massey's younger brother also joined the family business it caused friction between them and it quickly became clear that they could not work together for long.

Then the family business purchased an upmarket jewellery shop in Bramhall, Cheshire, which had gone into receivership. Massey discovered that the shop had one corporate account and provided a gold watch every month for the firm's long-service employees. It planted an idea in

his mind. He says: 'I thought it must be dead easy business because the corporate customer just ordered the watches automatically without us having to do anything.'

So in 1990, at the age of 26, he started up a tiny division in a room at the back of the shop to provide gold watches and clocks for companies to give to their employees as long-service awards. His father, however, was not optimistic. Massey says: 'He was happy for me to go ahead with it but he thought I was wasting my time.' Undaunted, Massey hired a secretary, spent £3,000 getting a brochure printed, and posted it out to all the big companies he could think of.

His first call was from Tarmac, whose long-service employees were given a choice of a traditional gift such as a clock or watch, or something from Dixon's, the electrical retailer. Massey was given the contact to provide the traditional gifts but soon realised that he wasn't getting any orders. He says: 'I rang up the human resources manager and said nobody is ordering anything. She told me they were all going to Dixons.'

It was at that point Massey had his big idea. It was one which would transform the business. He says: 'I realised that to succeed as a provider I had to offer a range of branded products, some form of brochure and as much administration as we could provide to the human resources department of a firm.'

So he started including goods such as televisions and cameras in the range he offered corporate clients. By 1992 he was making sales of £300,000 a year and had set up his own company to target the long-service award market.

Then he got a huge break. Massey was given the opportunity to tender for a £1-million contract from British Rail to provide their long-service and retirement awards. But he realised that they might be reluctant to give him the account if they knew how small his business was so he decided to give them the impression his was a much bigger company than it really was. He says: 'When they visited us, we emptied the shop completely of jewellery and we just put the products on show we had tendered for, so it looked like the showroom for a long-service award company, not a jeweller's shop. They loved it.'

Fact file

Date of birth: 8 May 1964

Marital status: married with four children

Qualifications: none

Interests: cycling, eating out

Personal philosophy: 'Treat every day as being really valuable because if you work out how many you get, it is not that many.'

Out of 14 tenders he won the account. He says: 'I thought this is it, we have cracked it.'

The only problem was that having won the contract he had just four months to transform his business into one that was capable of delivering the service he had promised. He says: 'I had no staff and no warehouse and the business wasn't computerised. All I had was an office and a phone.' Massey rented an office suite and started recruiting staff, and by time the contract began at the start of 1993 he was ready.

But he had another hurdle to overcome. As he had no track record, suppliers refused to give him credit even though he was buying hundreds of thousands of pounds' worth of stock. Within six weeks he had a major cash flow problem. To make matters worse British Rail announced a voluntary retirement scheme ahead of privatisation which meant it needed lots of gifts to give leaving staff. By April it had already exceeded its anticipated £1-million annual budget.

He says: 'When I went to the Post Office to collect the orders each morning they gave me a sack full of them. It was exhausting because there was so much pressure from every side. I had to stop for a nap while driving home one day because I felt overwhelmed by it all.'

Fortunately, crisis was averted when British Rail offered to pay Massey within seven days instead of up to two months later.

Within the space of a year turnover had jumped from £300,000 to £2.5 million. British Rail extended the contract for another two years and Massey took on more clients, providing each of them with brochures individualised with their own corporate identity.

He says: 'Our competitors were dinosaurs, they just wanted to supply traditional products. So we told people we could provide them with a brochure, we could provide them with a massive range of merchandise. We added loads of value.'

Massey had a nagging fear that the size of the overall market was shrinking because he knew that fewer and fewer people were staying in the same job for 25 years. But one day he was asked to provide an award for an employee who had achieved five years' service and realised that the nature of the market had changed.

He says: 'I discovered that companies love to reward staff because it pays. They don't have to spend a lot of money rewarding someone for five years' service but it creates a feel-good factor which really works for the company. Nowadays staff retention is such a major issue that in many businesses they reward service from five years upwards.' He adds: 'I realised that there was a really good market out there. The traditional providers had all given up and so I thought, well, let's really go for this.'

He started by introducing Aspirations, a brochure which offered greater choice and gave each product a points value. That meant that recipients could choose several gifts up to the value of the points they were awarded, and if their choice of gift exceed their points allowance, they could purchase additional points at the same discounted rate.

It was an inspired idea. Soon 60 per cent of all recipients were buying additional points, creating an unexpected new source of revenue.

Then Massey started managing the administration of the scheme for companies, sending out the gifts to the recipients directly on behalf of the chief executive or chairman.

He says: 'We were always looking for ways to add value to the process to ensure that nobody could steal the business from us. My fear was always that somebody bigger would twig what we were doing and take it away from me.'

Over the past two years he has also focused increasingly on the potential offered by the growing incentive and motivation market and hired specialist staff from the sector to help him. He says: 'I knew that to keep the corporate side of the business growing we had to move away from just being a long-service award provider. So we now provide gifts for incentive, motivation and reward.'

The constant stream of innovations paid off. The business has grown by an average of 36 per cent every year since 1992 and in 2006 is expected to have sales of £20 million. Cottrills now provides an awards scheme for 700 blue chip companies including Tesco and Ford and retains 98 per cent of its clients from year to year.

Now 42, Massey says he has been driven by a desire to prove to everyone that his idea really could work. He says: 'Initially it was to prove to my dad that I could do it. I also got such a buzz from dealing with big businesses such as ICI. I still get nervous before meetings and when I walk out with a new account it really does give me a kick.'

In his view becoming a successful entrepreneur is all about making the most of any opportunity that comes along. He says: 'I am tempted to say that finding a good business idea is about finding something which is niche that you can grow and develop. But really you have just got to do your absolute best in every way. I stumbled across an area that any jeweller in the country could have found, but there were a lot of complacent suppliers out there. What we did was turn ourselves into a category killer.'

14

Sally Preston
Founder of Babylicious

Sally Preston's parents always hoped that she would become a doctor. But when she started studying for science A levels she realised she had no chance of getting the grades she needed. She says: 'It became really obvious to me after about two weeks of A level physics that I couldn't understand a word of it.' So she looked around for another path to follow and after doing work experience with a dietician decided to take a degree in food sciences instead.

After graduating she got a job with Marks & Spencer in their ready meals department. She ended up staying 11 years, rising to become senior food technologist.

But she never really fitted into the corporate world. Preston says: 'I was ambitious but also non-conforming. On my first day I turned up with a fluorescent pink tin briefcase and was asked to stop using it because it wasn't sufficiently corporate.'

So in 1999, at the age of 33 and with two small children, she left Marks & Spencer to start up her own food consultancy, advising companies on factory development. Just two

months into her new role however, she hit upon her big idea – to start up a business selling frozen baby food in ice-cube trays so that parents could use as much or as little as they needed to feed their babies.

She says: 'When I had my first child I cooked quite a lot of food for her myself and froze the rest in ice-cube trays like mothers were being advised to in magazines. But I found the whole process a bit of a chore. When I was at home not working I really wanted to do things with Hannah and meet other mums, rather than spend hours making food and pureeing it and putting it in ice-cube trays.'

The effort of cooking got even harder when she had her second child. She says: 'When I had my son Jack he never even got a taste of home-made food because by then I had a toddler charging around and I had gone back to work. I wanted to give my children good healthy food but I didn't want the hassle that went with it. And I thought there had to be something better than baby food from jars.'

Before Preston could put her plan into action however, her world fell apart. Her marriage collapsed in acrimonious circumstances and she and the children had to leave the family house to live in rented accommodation. Just four months later she was diagnosed with skin cancer after discovering a mole on her thigh. All thoughts of starting up her own business were abandoned while she underwent treatment and tried to put her life back together.

Two years later, however, things looked much more promising. She had a new partner and decided that her big idea might be worth looking at again. She says: 'It seemed such an obvious idea to me. I couldn't understand why no-one else had done it.'

Her new partner agreed to pay the household bills while she started her baby food business so Preston gave up her food consultancy and got to work. She says: 'I thought, what have I got to lose? From day one I had very big ambitions. I decided I didn't want to make the product myself at home and supply the local deli, I wanted to create a brand that would be sold through retailers and have national distribution.'

She started creating recipes in her kitchen for babies aged from 4 months to 12 months, based on dishes such as chicken casserole and fisherman's pie, which were favourites of her

Fact file

Date of birth: 11 October 1964

Marital status: divorced with two children

Qualifications: BSc (Hons) in food science from South Bank Polytechnic

Interests: socialising, aerobics, running, skiing

Personal philosophy: 'Don't think too long and hard about things. Follow your first instinct.'

own children. She says: 'I gave them to the mothers I knew at the school gates to try and said: "What do you reckon to this?" It wasn't very scientific – there was no market research or consumer panels.'

Then she found a factory in Leicester that agreed to make the meals for her. Just as she had originally envisaged, the food was frozen in ice-cube trays so parents could use as much or as little as they needed for their babies.

But she did not have much luck getting a bank to agree to lend her money. She says: 'Every single bank said it was such an obvious idea that they couldn't understand why nobody else had done it – and therefore there must be a reason why no one else had done it. But I think in fact the most obvious ideas are the good ideas and you shouldn't shy away from one just because it is so glaringly obvious. You don't need to be contrived and make things up, the good ideas are all there.'

So she remortgaged her house to raise the £55,000 she needed to get the business off the ground and hired a design company to help her create a brand for her product. The result was Babylicious and within weeks the supermarket chain Waitrose had agreed to stock it in 27 stores – on the condition that Preston delivered the products to the stores herself. Undaunted, she promptly bought herself a 1.5 tonne freezer van.

But before Preston could start supplying the stores, the business hit a major setback. When she tried to register the name Babylicious as a trademark she discovered someone else had beaten her to it and lodged the same name and classification just 11 days earlier. With the threat of litigation looming Preston had no option but to change the name to Tastylicious. She says: 'It was not just the packaging we had to change, it was all the corporate stationery, the website, the marketing materials, absolutely everything.'

However, Preston was not about to give up without a fight. She says: 'I was not prepared to accept that this company had suddenly, out of nowhere, just come along and taken my idea. It had to be more than just coincidence.'

She decided to contest the application and in the process discovered that it had been lodged by a woman she knew. Nine months later the court accepted that the rival application had been made in bad faith. Preston was allowed to use the Babylicious name again and promptly changed everything back. However, in total the rebranding cost £30,000.

And her problems were not over yet. In 2002 the same woman started ringing up Preston's business contracts and spreading malicious rumours about the company, falsely claiming that it was being investigated. Preston realised something was going on when people started cancelling meetings and advertisements. She took the woman to court and ended up paying out £10,000 in lawyer's fees before dropping the case. She says: 'I was advised by my lawyer to take the moral high ground and walk away. It was a very difficult thing to do but I had to focus on the business.' She ended up having to borrow £25,000 from her parents just to keep the business afloat.

Preston also faced an uphill battle persuading retailers to install freezers in the baby section of their stores for her products instead of putting them in the freezer section.

By 2003, though, things started to turn a corner. Babylicious won several industry awards and received lots of publicity when it was discovered that Victoria Beckham fed the food to her son Romeo.

Two years ago Preston raised £1 million from private investors in return for an equity stake of 25 per cent. The company's products are now stocked by Asda, Tesco and Sainsbury's and sales in 2006 are expected to be around £4 million.

In contrast to some entrepreneurs, Preston says she has only ever really had one idea for starting up a business – this one. She says: 'I just had this one idea and went for it. This was the only one. I thought, I can do that.'

Despite the setbacks she has had to endure over the past few years, she says the effort has been worth it. She says: 'This is just such an obvious business opportunity that if I hadn't done it I would have been forever frustrated that somebody else had. I wanted to prove that I could do it. And I wanted to be in control of my life. When it is my son's school sports day, I know I can be there. I don't have to ask anybody's permission.'

15

Will Ramsay
Founder of the Affordable Art Fair

Every March and October thousands of people make their way to a marquee in London's Battersea Park to attend the Affordable Art Fair, a four-day event where visitors can pick up original works of art from as little £50. Now in its seventh year, the Affordable Art Fair is the vision of Will Ramsay, who was determined to find a way of making art more accessible to people who would not normally buy it.

Born and brought up in Scotland, Ramsay first became interested in art while at school when he studied art and art history. He went on to study geography at Newcastle University and then spent five years in the army serving with the Royal Scots Dragoon Guards.

However, art continued to hold a fascination for him and when he left the army he would often cycle around London on his bike visiting art galleries. But he found them intimidating places and would often get a frosty reception.

He says: 'I felt that I wasn't being welcomed or looked after or helped to learn more. There was a fear factor about

going into a gallery. There would be no one else in there and you could hear your footsteps on the wooden floor and you'd feel really self-conscious. I felt I wasn't being treated as a potential customer who was there to be nurtured.'

He also hated the way that galleries would only display the work of one artist at a time. He says: 'I thought it was bizarre that you could go into a shoe shop and find a whole selection of different shoes but if you walked into a gallery and didn't like the work by the artist they were showing then you would walk away disappointed.'

Before leaving the army Ramsay decided he wanted to set up his own business. On a visit to the United States he tried frozen yoghurt and briefly toyed with the idea of selling it in the UK. He says: 'I remember thinking it would be fantastic over here, why don't we have it here already?'

Then one day in 1994 Ramsay had his big idea. Inspired by his love of art, he decided to set up a gallery of his own. It would display work by up to 15 living artists at a time and would be a place where people could buy affordable art in a relaxed atmosphere with friendly staff and music playing in the background. He based his business model on the wine market, where he could see that companies such as Oddbins had prospered by making wine more accessible to potential customers.

Ramsay says: 'Art and wine are very similar in that they are both areas that people feel they should know about and feel embarrassed if they don't. Thirty years ago the wine market was really just geared towards people who knew about wine and knew what they wanted to stock their cellar. But now it has grown to include much more of the population who want to drink wine but who don't know much about it and don't want to spend a huge amount of money.' He adds: 'Oddbins and Majestic Wines have got round that by putting helpful labels on the back of the bottle and by being user-friendly. I thought the same sort of thing might be possible with art.'

Excited by his idea, Ramsay persuaded his bank to give him an overdraft of £100,000 and found an old Victorian warehouse in Parson's Green in South West London, to turn into a gallery. Then he visited student shows and artist

Fact file

Date of birth: 22 February 1969

Marital status: married with two children

Qualifications: BA in geography from Newcastle University

Interests: horse riding, amateur jockey

Personal philosophy: 'You have only one life so live it to the full. No one on their death bed says: "I wish I had spent more time in the office."'

studios to find work to display, deciding right from the start to sell only work by living artists so that any sales would help them earn a living from their art. He called his gallery Will's Art Warehouse.

The first few months were hard going. Ramsay spent £96,000 of the £100,000 overdraft before the business started to become cash positive and the debt began to come down. In the end the business was saved when he discovered that he could make money by hiring out the gallery for private parties after a friend pointed out that it was the perfect size.

However, other ideas didn't work. Ramsay opened two more galleries in Notting Hill and Windsor but they were not a success and after six months he had to close them down. He explains: 'The problem was stock. We had to move the exhibitions round from gallery to galley and so if a customer said they liked a painting which was there last week, it would take a while to get it back. Then when the customer eventually came in they would say they didn't like it as much as they remembered. It was a nightmare.'

But Ramsay was still convinced that his vision of selling affordable art in a relaxed atmosphere could appeal to a wider audience. So seven years ago he hit upon the idea of holding an annual art fair where dozens of galleries could exhibit their work in the same place.

There was already a fair for contemporary art held in London each year, but every time Ramsay had applied for space to exhibit work there he had been rejected. Even worse, on his latest attempt he was erroneously sent some transparencies of art that belonged to a gallery in Dublin. It got him thinking. He says: 'The transparencies were lovely and I thought that if they were turning down this kind of quality then they were obviously getting so many applications that they couldn't send the right images back to the right galleries.'

He also quizzed some friends who had attended the art fair and asked them what they thought. He says: 'They said they loved it but that they couldn't afford anything. The problem was that in fact they could have afforded lots but nothing was priced – and the one picture they were brave enough to ask the price of was £20,000.'

He asked a few gallery owners what they thought of his plan of setting up an art fair which was not intimidating for people who knew very little about art. They thought it was a good idea and so Ramsay got to work. He says: 'I have always been someone who has organised things. I used to organise parties at university. I just loved it.'

The first Affordable Art Fair was held in London in 1999 and was an instant success, attracting 87 galleries and 10,000 visitors, who between them spent £1 million on art.

Ramsay now organises two Affordable Art Fairs a year in London as well as fairs in Bristol, New York, Sydney and Melbourne and he plans to hold more in Europe and the United States. So far more than £50 million of art has been sold at the fairs in total and more than 250,000 people have visited worldwide.

He explains the appeal: 'Having loads of small galleries in one place takes away the fear factor for people. They know that everything is going to be under £3,000 and that in an environment where there are loads of people they can lose themselves in the throng.'

He adds: 'We insist on everything being priced and we have demonstrations and lectures and so it makes it easy for people. They can see 130 galleries in a day which would take them several weekends to go and see elsewhere.'

Ramsay, who now runs his business from Scotland, thinks that in some ways not having a degree in art actually helped him find the vision for his business. He says: 'It was probably because I came from the standpoint of someone who hadn't got a degree that I saw that potential. If I had got a degree I probably would have felt I knew everything and felt part of the art world, and I wouldn't have noticed the opportunity.'

Now 37, he says becoming an entrepreneur has given him the freedom to structure his life in the way he chooses. He says: 'I didn't want to work in an office in the city for 30 years, I wanted to be able to choose where I work, when I work – and one day to be able to change tack and do something else, perhaps retire early and do charity work. We have only got one life and you have got to live it to the full.'

16

Ian Wilson
Founder of WEXAS

Ian Wilson first discovered a burning desire to travel at the age of nine when his family emigrated from Nottingham to New Zealand. Within weeks Wilson, his brother and his mother desperately wanted to return home to England. But his father, who suffered from recurring bouts of malaria, had been advised to seek a warmer climate for his health, and so they stayed. Perhaps not surprisingly, by the time he was 13 Wilson's hobby was collecting travel brochures from around the world.

In the end Wilson was not able to return to the UK until he was 22 after he had graduated from Auckland University with a degree in French and got a place to study for a doctorate in political philosophy at Oxford University.

His mother was ambitious for him to succeed but Wilson soon discovered that he preferred academic life. 'My mother wanted me to be the chairman of ICI and failing that, a diplomat or a lawyer. But I didn't know what I was going to do next – and I didn't have any particular desire to find out quickly. I found I was quite academic and that I liked finding out new facts and making discoveries and evolving theories.'

After graduating from Oxford he travelled around the United States for a couple of months and then got a job with an advertising agency J Walter Thompson. But his heart was not in it and after a year there, at the age of 26, he decided to look around for another way of making a living. He says: 'I wanted to find a way out of climbing up the corporate ladder.'

His first idea was to try to get a novel published which he had written while at university. When that failed he toyed with the idea of helping to promote the Cape Verde Islands as a tourist destination. The government there had hired a Belgian professor of urban planning to advise them how to do this. So Wilson went to Brussels to talk to the professor with the intention of becoming the UK marketing representative for the Cape Verde Island.

However, it was not to be. Wilson says: 'I translated a lot of documents from Portuguese into English, but the whole project collapsed and never got off the ground.'

It was while he was sitting in the garden talking to a friend from university one summer evening in 1970 that Wilson came up with his big idea. The two of them had a bet about who could start up the most successful travel company, so Wilson decided to start up a travel club which would offer university students, nurses and teachers cheap flights in return for an annual membership fee of £1.25. He says: 'Somehow the idea popped up as though it was the obvious thing to do. It was a distillation of different things from different directions.'

He called his club WUNEXAS, which stood for World Universities Expeditionary Association, and paid for his first mail shot with £150 borrowed on his overdraft. He got a friend who worked in the printing department at J Walter Thompson to print posters advertising the club for him during his lunch hour. Then in his own lunch hour he compiled lists of student unions and nurses' homes from directories in the library at J Walter Thompson. He says: 'I sent a poster round to the secretaries of the student unions and nurses' homes asking them if they could put it on their notice board.'

Fact file

Date of birth: 15 November 1943

Marital status: twice married with three children

Qualifications: MA in French. Doctor of Philosophy (DPhil) in political philosophy from Oxford University

Interests: Collecting early New Zealand maps, surfing, sailing, diving, skiing

Personal philosophy: 'The fight goes on. Every time there is adversity in life you must always fight your way back and keep going and keep on trying.'

Then he got to work negotiating cheap deals from flight wholesalers. He says: 'I would go round to see the consolidators in their little offices with a wodge of membership forms in my hand and persuade them I could guarantee them a certain amount of bookings. Our members were buying tickets for £250 which had a price on them of £400.'

To start with Wilson continued to work full time at the advertising agency while working on his travel club at home at evenings and weekends. After nine months however, in 1971, the club was going so well that left his job to work on it full time. As a result he instantly tripled his salary.

In the first year his club, the name of which he soon shortened to WEXAS, had attracted 1,200 members. By the second year this had risen to 2,000 and the company moved to rented offices above a restaurant in Knightsbridge, where Wilson also started providing grants to university expeditions from profits. He explains: 'I wasn't ambitious to be rich, I was ambitious to do something fulfilling – and for me fulfilment meant doing something useful. I didn't have any great material aspirations.'

Indeed, after four years of running the club, at the age of 30, Wilson decided to take an even more radical step – he appointed a managing director to run the company so that he could spend four months of every year travelling the world. He has run the company that way ever since, often taking his wife and two children with him on his trips, which usually take in surfing, diving and sailing.

In 1976 the business hit a bad patch. Wilson opened a second office in New York but within two years had to close it, losing £35,000. However, he is philosophical about the event. 'It wasn't all a bad experience because I got to surf in California and write a novel. It was published in America and was quite successful.'

Then in 1982 the office burnt down while Wilson was surfing in the Turks and Caicos islands, completely undoing the company's recent relaunch aimed at boosting sales. 'We all had to wear overalls because the place was filthy and blackened, and everyone worked from one room on one phone line for several weeks. Customers couldn't get through to us.' To make matters worse, the insurance company refused to pay out the full amount Wilson believed he was entitled to, leaving the company £80,000 out of pocket.

Despite the setbacks, however, WEXAS has continued to thrive, attracting older wealthier clients as they have aged with the company. It now offers hotels, cruises and car hire as well as flights and has become a tour operator, a move which has enabled it to withstand competition from low cost airlines and the internet. WEXAS now has 35,000 members, employs 130 staff and has annual sales of £40 million which produce a gross profit of £6.5 million.

For Wilson having a club and members has been a key element of the way the company operates. He says: 'I never saw myself as a travel agent, I saw myself as a marketing person getting membership. Indeed, for many years the whole thrust of WEXAS was membership rather than travel sales, to the point where until 1990 our main source of income was probably subscriptions.'

Now 62, Wilson thinks that having a club with members has been both a blessing and a curse. He says: 'I think having a subscription membership has limited the size the company can grow to because only a certain market will be happy to pay for the service. But paradoxically it has enabled me to have the free life I wanted because size hinders you. If you have a company of a certain size then someone else can run it for you and that leaves you free to run your life and do the things you want to do.'

He is particularly proud of having been able to combine creating a successful business with living his life as he chooses. He says: 'I don't measure success just by size and profitability, I measure success by whether I am feeling fulfilled by what I am doing. I can't see the point of people working every hour they have to become the biggest and the best and the richest if it is only to suddenly die of a heart attack having had no time to enjoy it all. I think you should enjoy it while you have the chance.'

17

Karen Darby
Founder of Simply Switch

For many people, getting a job in telesales ends up being the most miserable experience of their life. For Karen Darby however, it was an epiphany. 'I loved it,' she says. 'It didn't feel like work at all. I couldn't believe I was getting paid for talking to people on the phone. It was like getting money for old rope.'

The second youngest of five children, Darby was brought up on a council estate in Mitcham, Surrey, by a father who was unemployed most of the time and a mother who worked part time as a waitress.

'I was always looking for ways to make money because we didn't have much,' she says. 'I worked in a fish shop and a launderette, I delivered newspapers, I used to scour the streets for lemonade bottles and take them back to the shops for the deposit. At one time I had four different jobs on the go.'

Darby left school at 16 with one O level and started work in a factory. But she hated it so much that after two months she left with no other job to go to. 'It was unbearable,' she

says. 'It taught me a useful lesson in life – never do a job just for the pay packet.'

She then got a job in telesales selling advertising space for newspapers and discovered that she loved it. After two years she moved to Capital Radio to sell airtime and later went to work for a sales-promotion agency.

Then in 1983, at the age of 22, she and a colleague decided to set up a call centre of their own, with £30,000 provided by a private investor. 'People said I was brave but I didn't really see it that way,' she says. 'I hadn't got a lot to lose.' She opened a call centre in a shop in Norbury, South London, and got on the phone. 'I would call up the marketing directors of huge consumer-goods companies and drag them down to our shop to see what telemarketing could do for their brand,' she says. 'We sold everything from baked beans to computers.'

After seven years the company had 200 staff and sales of £4 million. But Darby was pregnant with her second child and decided it was time to do something different. 'It had got to the stage where I was ready for a change,' she says.

She sold her share for £1.6 million, but the buyer went bust soon afterwards and Darby got just £500,000. She is philosophical about the loss. 'If something goes wrong or doesn't work out, I always think there's a reason for it and that something good will come of it,' she says.

She bought a house for cash with the money and started working from home as a telesales trainer for other call centres. But after 10 years of doing this, at the age of 42 and having had her third baby, she decided she really wanted to set up another business of her own. She says: 'I was earning really good money as a consultant and trainer but it wasn't increasing my net worth because I was only earning when I was actually working. The difference between doing that and having a business is that when you have your own business you can make money when you sleep.'

Her first thought was to start up a training business of her own. She says: 'A lot of the training industry is made up of small independent companies so I decided to raise some funds and buy lots of training companies to create this huge training empire.' But after talking to several banks about her idea she discovered that they were not willing to put up the

Fact file

Date of birth: 30 August 1960

Marital status: married three times with three children

Qualifications: One O level

Interests: spending time with family, baking cakes, writing jokes

Personal philosophy: 'You will never get rich working for someone else.'

money she needed. So she abandoned the idea and started thinking again.

Her next idea was a concept she called Pocket Franchise to help employees become entrepreneurs within the companies they worked for by giving them an equity stake in the ideas they thought up. She says: 'I thought it was a great idea. I couldn't sleep and it completely obsessed me.'

She realised, however, that it could take forever to get company directors to adopt her venture. 'Big companies liked the idea but I think it made them a bit nervous. If you have to sell it in to a big corporation where it has to be signed off at board level then you are on a very long burn there, and I just didn't have the patience. I wanted it now.'

It was then that she had her big idea. Still working as a consultant, Darby was asked to advise a call centre that was trying to attract new customers for two energy companies in the newly deregulated gas and electricity markets. The company was cold-calling householders at home but was having very little success. She says: 'I suggested that instead of phoning people and trying to ram the product down their throats they should find out which was the best supplier for that particular customer and then sell the contract back to the energy company. It just seemed blindingly obvious to me. I thought it was a win–win situation.'

The client was not interested in her solution to the problem. But as she walked back to her car Darby realised that she was. She says: 'I was walking from their office to the car park when I thought: "Ooh that is a good idea, maybe there could be some mileage in it." And the more I thought about it, the more it wouldn't go away. It captured me emotionally as well as intellectually. It was absolutely right for the moment and it was simple. Anybody could understand the concept and it didn't take 20 minutes to explain.'

She started researching her idea and discovered that although there were some internet-based companies that gave people the ability to check gas and electricity prices and switch suppliers online, there were no telephone-based services, which she was convinced would work better.

She says: 'The market actually was a dot com business but we decided to come in with an old-fashioned way of doing it, by phone, because I thought that people would like the human contact a telephone service can offer. They want to speak to somebody who can answer their questions and allay their fears, who can reassure them that if they switch suppliers their garden path is not going to be dug up.'

She took the summer off to write a business plan and asked a colleague, Alistair Tillen, to join her as a partner. Then she went out looking for investors.

She tried to find a wealthy private individual but, when that did not work, she approached a firm of venture capitalists, Bridges Community Ventures. It liked her idea and agreed to invest £125,000 in the company in return for a 35 per cent equity stake. Darby remortgaged her house for £17,000, her partner put in £23,000, and the pair were in business.

The idea behind the new company, Simply Switch, was to work out for customers the cheapest energy supplier for their needs. If the customer decided to change to the recommended supplier, Simply Switch would earn a fixed fee from the energy company. The service was advertised through partnerships with newspapers, charities and retailers.

It was hard in the beginning to persuade the energy suppliers to take part in the scheme. And Simply Switch had to take a financial hit when one went bust owing it money.

But slowly the idea took off. Simply Switch now takes more than 1,000 calls a day from people looking for the cheapest energy deal and has expanded into offering advice on the cheapest phone company, broadband service and credit cards.

'All our customers call us because they are interested, and that makes a big difference,' says Darby. 'People don't like the idea of being sold to.'

The company now has 60 staff and is expected to have sales of £6 million in 2006. Darby also hopes to float it on the AIM listed market.

'I like getting my own way,' says Darby. 'If somebody says something can't be done, I like to show them that it can be. I am quite competitive.'

Now 45, Darby says she is motivated by the desire to make her mark. 'I don't just want to have on my tombstone: "Here lies Karen Darby, she was quite good on the phone." It is not enough for me. You can have millions of ideas but unless you have got the energy and the passion and the commitment and drive to actually make it happen then they just remain ideas. I want to make a contribution in life and do something of value. It would be nice to leave something behind.'

18

Guy Schanschieff
Founder of Bambino Mio

Guy Schanschieff found the initial inspiration for his big idea at the Taj Mahal. He got chatting to a tourist from the United States and when he mentioned that he wanted to start up his own business and was looking for inspiration, the man told him about nappy laundry services in New York which would collect and wash reusable nappies for customers.

They continued their conversation over dinner and by the time the evening ended Schanschieff had decided to start up a similar enterprise of his own back in the UK. He says: 'It started me thinking. It seemed like such a good idea.'

Schanschieff had always loved organising things. Brought up in Northamptonshire, at the age of seven he put on a charity jumble sale in the village where he lived. He says: 'I got somebody to type up a piece of paper saying "Jumble Wanted" and took it around the village. I can still remember the buzz I got seeing a massive queue of people waiting to get in.'

He also put on plays with his brothers and friends during the school holidays, converting the attic of the big old rectory

where they lived into a makeshift theatre. From the age of 18 he took theatre productions to the Edinburgh Festival with a group of friends for three years. He says: 'They didn't let me anywhere near the stage. For me it was all about the organisation and making it happen against the odds.'

When he left school Schanschieff went to Leicester polytechnic to do a degree in business studies and then joined a large accountancy firm, following in the footsteps of his accountant father. But it was not a wise move. He says: 'I was not particularly good and I was hugely bored.'

Fortunately, his girlfriend Jo had recently been made redundant and suggested they both went travelling for several months. Schanschieff agreed, in the hope that he might find inspiration for a business along the way.

Their first stop was India and just three weeks into their trip they met the US tourist at the Taj Mahal. Schanschieff says: 'We had already been thinking about setting up a laundry service which washed and ironed shirts for people in the City and so the nappy idea seemed such a good idea we largely closed ourselves off to other ideas at that point.'

They continued their travels to Sydney in Australia where Schanschieff talked to more people about the idea of setting up a reusable nappy laundry service. The idea continued to grow on them and so when they returned to the UK in 1992 he and Jo started a nappy laundering service of their own. They ran it from the front room of their home in Northampton and got local laundries to wash the nappies they collected from customers.

It was hard work. He says: 'It was very slow. Between September, which was when we started, and Christmas we got 13 customers.'

They gradually gained more customers and got more business by offering a rugby and football kit laundry business. They were also appointed distributor for a US company that made nappy covers.

After two years, however, the business still only had 250 customers and Schanschieff had realised that the laundry service was never going to be a big money spinner. But he remained convinced that modern-style reusable nappies, which were a big improvement on traditional terry nappies, had tremendous potential to take off in a big way.

Fact file

Date of birth: 2 January 1966

Marital status: married with three children

Qualifications: BA (Hons) in business studies from Leicester Polytechnic

Interests: running a cricket club

Personal philosophy: 'A man's reach should always exceed his grasp.'

So when in 1997 he heard that a former customer who had planned to start up a mail order business selling reusable nappies had changed her mind, he moved fast. He took over the name she had chosen for her company, Bambino Mio, all the stock and the brochures she had printed, and he was in business.

A few months later the decision to close the nappy laundry business was effectively made for him when the laundry he used decided they didn't want to wash dirty nappies any more. Schanschieff says: 'Nappies are not the nicest things to wash and we had nowhere else to go to. So overnight we decided to stop.' He and Jo, now his wife, started selling their reusable Bambino Mio nappies to independent baby shops and advertising in the back of baby magazines.

Once again the business was slow to take off. But this time Schanschieff was convinced he had found a winner. He says: 'A lot of people thought what I was trying to do was mad and that no one would use reusable nappies. There is a perception by parents that they are hard work and a hassle. But I thought we could create a strong brand that parents wanted to buy into. Reusable nappies have such a strong benefit to parents but they have never been properly marketed.'

The first store that agreed to stock his nappies was a small independent shop in Milton Keynes. Persuading the bigger stores to take his nappies, however, proved a lot harder and in 2001 the business hit a crisis. The company made a loss of £100,000 on sales of £700,000.

Schanschieff says: 'That was our lowest point. It hit us pretty hard. Everything had fallen apart with the company we were distributing for in America, which meant that we weren't getting the stock we needed of nappy covers, which was our key product. And we had a huge amount of back orders because the first nappies we sourced ourselves from China had been delayed. I have always been able to find a way out of difficulties but this time there didn't seem as though there was a way out.'

He decided to bring in a new national accounts manager to get more shops to stock Bambino Mio's nappies. It worked. Bambino Mio products are now stocked by several big high street retailers including John Lewis and Babies 'R' Us and are sold in 50 countries.

Sales in 2006 are expected to reach £3 million and Schanschieff estimates that 4.2 per cent of all babies in the UK now use Bambino Mio nappies some or all of the time.

He says: 'Five years ago parents who used reusable nappies were regarded as a bit off the wall. But it has become far more normal.'

Schanschieff, who together with his wife still owns 100 per cent of the company, thinks the secret of his success has been to stay completely focused. He says: 'I always had a blind belief that it was going to succeed. I am very passionate about what I do because I think there is so much that can be achieved. For anybody who has a desire to start their own business, the greatest thing you can ever have in terms of an idea is something that somebody hasn't done before. To be able to find a product which nobody was exploiting and then to grow it and develop it, as I have been able to, is fantastic.'

He thinks that the essence of a good business idea is finding a niche product or service which has a good story to tell. He says: 'What we have done it taken a product category – reusable nappies – which had almost been forgotten, and then applied 21st-century marketing and business techniques to it. It didn't have to be reusable nappies, it could have been any product – for me it is all about how you focus on it and bring all the marketing and distribution and everything else to it. It is about making sure that all the pieces of the jigsaw fit.'

He thinks that for him at least, leaving his job to go travelling was a good way of coming up with a good idea. He says: 'The travelling path seems to be much more well trodden in the last few years. But I would still advocate it because you are away from all the day-to-day influences that you normally have so it gives you the chance to look at things from a different angle.'

Now 40 with three children, he still cannot resist organising things. For the past 20 years he has run his own cricket club and every year organises overseas tours to play teams in places such as Spain and Malta. 'I have always been one of these people who will go off and organise things. I am a great organiser.'

As for Bambino Mio, he says: 'The motivation is definitely not money, it is to prove it can be done – and that not only will I do it, but I will do it better than anybody else. I have always operated in a fairly competitive environment, whether at boarding school or within the family.'

There have, however, been a few drawbacks to his choice of business. He says: 'It is often a conversation stopper. Friends at dinner parties will make an apology for using disposable nappies. I am sure my children tell people I am a lawyer or an accountant.'

19

Lucy Barker

Founder of Barker Brooks Media

Lucy Barker was having a drink in her local pub one evening when she happened to overhear the conversation the man at the next table was having with his wife. The man was local public relations figure Paul Sowerby and he was talking about how he planned to set up a publishing division of his company. Barker says: 'The following day I knocked on his door and told him I was the answer to his prayers. Fortunately, he thought it was very funny and offered me a job.'

Born and brought up in West Yorkshire, Barker was privately educated but did not enjoy school and at 16 left to go to sixth form college. Within two months, however, she realised that her heart was not in that either. She says: 'The headmaster called me in and told me I should get out there into the big wide world.'

She got a job in London as an office junior in a public relations company and then became a production assistant for music producer Tim Rice, who was putting on his musical *Chess*. Then she helped two friends start up a student magazine called *Rasp*. She says: 'The name doesn't mean anything

at all but we told people that rasping was American slang for chatting. Or if we were talking to somebody from education we would say that *Rasp* stood for Real Answers to Student Prospects.' The magazine was fairly successful and made enough for the three of them to live on modestly for five years until they sold it for £36,000.

Barker, by now 25, then went on holiday in Egypt where she met and fell in love with a Frenchman. She went to live in Paris with him where they got married and had a child. When they moved back to Yorkshire however the marriage fell apart and Barker was left to bring up her daughter on her own. She supported the two of them by doing sales jobs, but it was a struggle. They lived in a hut on a farm with no heating or hot water.

It was then that she met Paul Sowerby in the pub. He took her on to help him publish a small weekly newsletter for the Law Society in Leeds, the only project his fledging publishing company had.

Just six months later in 1999, however, Sowerby was offered a job elsewhere and closed the company down. But Barker, then 29, realised she had stumbled upon her big idea. She decided to set up a publishing company of own, starting with the newsletter. She says: 'It was just a four-page stapled thing which was typed by the Law Society secretary but I thought it should be a proper magazine. My brother is a lawyer and I thought the legal profession might need it.'

Sowerby agreed to let Barker keep the newsletter provided that she bought the furniture and computers from him. So she borrowed £10,000 from the bank and got to work.

It was perhaps inevitable she would end up starting up her own business. Both her parents were entrepreneurial – her father designed and produced greetings cards and her mother ran her own successful modelling agency. Indeed her great uncle, who also owned his own business, once wrote a book called *How To Make a Million*.

She says: 'I have always wanted to start up my own business. I think you are born with it. Some people are just not suited to working for other people.'

The Law Society in Leeds agreed to let Barker keep any money she made from advertising, providing that adverts accounted for no more than 40 per cent of the publication. She says: 'To start with the profit was tiny but as we got better

Fact file

Date of birth: 13 November 1967

Marital status: separated with one child

Qualifications: eight O levels

Interests: horse riding, walking, playing the piano

Personal philosophy: 'Life shrinks or expands in proportion to one's courage.'

at producing a quality professional publication, suddenly the advertising revenue was there. It was amazing.'

Barker hired an editor to help her produce the magazine and incorporated the editor's surname Brooks into the name of the company. It was a generous but misguided move – within six months the editor had left. By that time, however, the name had stuck.

She also started paying several visits to the Law Society headquarters in London to discuss the possibility of producing more magazines for them. She says: 'I thought hang on a minute, there is a market here and there is absolutely no point in me sitting up in Harrogate producing one regional title when there is a lot to be gained from this relationship.'

The Law Society agreed and soon she was publishing several national magazines for them as well. She also started up magazines for other professional bodies in fields such accountancy and banking which already had an existing membership base.

She explains: 'I saw a huge gap in the market. I did a lot of research and I knew that if I produced a magazine for an organisation which already had members then I wouldn't need to find them myself. It would be a huge short cut.'

She also toyed with the idea of starting up a music magazine similar to *NME*, but was quickly talked out of it. She says: 'I had loads of dreadful ideas which I talked to family members about, and I got reactions ranging from hysterical laughter to people telling me I must be absolutely mad.'

Instead she started organising awards ceremonies linked to the magazines she produced, starting with the Yorkshire Lawyer Awards to recognise legal talent in Yorkshire.

After two years in business, however, things started to become unstuck. She says: 'We made the classic mistake of expanding far too quickly and taking on projects which were not profitable.'

Their offices were flooded four times in a year which destroyed the computers and forced the company to relocate to temporary offices. Then Barker found a lump in her breast while on a business trip to Brazil. She was diagnosed with breast cancer and told it was a very aggressive grade three tumour. She was 34. She says: 'The bottom dropped out of my world.'

The discovery, however, marked an unexpected turning point in her life. With both she and her business fighting for their lives she decided the only way forward was to win on both counts. She says: 'The day after I was diagnosed I decided that not only was I going to beat this thing and turn my health around – I was also going to use this as a massive opportunity to turn the business around. I thought, right, this is where my life starts. It was nothing to do with being brave. I needed to have something else to think about other than the possibility of dying.'

Barker began by promoting two employees to be directors so they could run the business while she was having chemotherapy. Then she ruthlessly axed the projects which were not making enough profit, cutting the company's ventures from 10 to 5. She explains: 'Just as the chemotherapy was there to stamp out all the cancer, I decided to stamp out all of the negative aspects of the company.'

Halfway through her chemotherapy treatment she also realised that the business needed a big injection of cash. So she remortgaged her house for £100,000 – and also put every penny of a £40,000 critical illness insurance payout straight into the business. She says: 'I remember my mother saying to me, aren't you even going to take out enough to go on holiday? I told her I hadn't got time.'

Her determination on both fronts paid off. After undergoing eight months of chemotherapy the cancer is now in remission, and the business is thriving. Barker has launched several new profitable magazines and events, most notably *Etc*, a magazine for A level students, to replace the ones she culled. She also produces a magazine for the British Racing Drivers club at Silverstone and recently bought the modelling agency and production company owned by her mother. As a result turnover is expected to be £5.5 million in 2006.

Now 38, Barker says: 'It is weird but for me getting cancer was the turning point in my life and for the business. In a way it has made me more successful. I am unbelievably proud of what I have achieved – but I still have a long way to go.'

She is clear about what motivates her. 'At the end of the day I am driven by the idea of making money because I know what it is like to have absolutely nothing and I never ever want to go back to that. For me profit is the most important thing.'

She thinks the secret of her success has been to ask for help: 'My big turning point was realising that there are other people that I could talk to. I realised I couldn't be good at everything so I should concentrate on the things that I am good at – and let other people do the things I was not good at.'

20

Richard Tang

Founder of Zen Internet

Richard Tang first discovered a passion for computers at the age of 13 when his school bought a Commodore computer for pupils to use. He says: 'I used to spend all my lunchtimes and breaks programming it. I was absolutely amazed by it. I had always been interested in building things and I loved the idea that you could take a computer that could not do anything and then programme it to do something useful and functional.'

Born and brought up in Rochdale with his two younger brothers by his Chinese father and English mother, by the time he was 15 Tang had bought a computer of his own with money earned selling pet food in the local market. He also formed a fictitious company, Zen Microsystems, so that computer suppliers would be fooled into sending him catalogues and data sheets about their products.

After taking a degree in computer systems at Salford University, Tang got a job designing computer hardware. While he was there he and a few colleagues would often head down to the local pub to dream about ways of making

their fortune. Tang says: 'We came up with all sorts of wild and wacky ideas. All of them were based around computers and the idea of developing a piece of software or hardware which we could sell.'

Nothing came of their discussions, however, and after four years and several promotions Tang realised that his heart was not in climbing the corporate ladder. He says: 'I could see my life mapped out ahead of me. I wanted to do something a bit different.'

So in 1993, at the age of 27, he gave up his job to travel around China and India for nine months. When he returned he decided to start up his own company designing computer software and hardware.

He hired a Portakabin in Birmingham to serve as an office and after three months of waiting for the phone to ring he managed to get some work writing software for a large company and planned to gradually take on more clients. But a few months into the contract Tang was having a drink in the pub with his younger brother Daniel when he hit upon a big idea that sounded a lot more exciting.

The two of them started talking about a new concept called the internet. Tang had only just heard of the internet and had never used it. But his brother was an academic and already used it at Cambridge University where he was doing a post-graduate degree in artificial intelligence. When Tang asked him whether he thought the internet would be a success, Daniel said he was convinced it would take off in a big way.

Inspired by his brother's enthusiasm Tang decided to start up a company that provided access to the internet, figuring that it was an opportunity he could not afford to miss. He also thought that it might be a much easier way to make money than writing software.

He says: 'The problem with software design is that every time you want to earn some more money you have to do some more work. Whereas I thought that if I set up a subscription-based service giving people access to the inter-net then once I had signed someone up the money would keep coming in and it would involve very little work. As an internet service provider I could create a situation where I would have subscriptions coming in every month – without actually doing very much.'

Fact file

Date of birth: 19 February 1966

Marital status: partnered

Qualifications: BEng in electronic computer systems from Salford University

Interests: windsurfing, paragliding, playing the piano

Personal philosophy: 'Make the most of life because time is precious.'

He persuaded friends and family to lend him £20,000 to get started. His brother did not want to be part of the business but agreed to spend six months building a network for him which would connect his customers to the internet. He created a network by attaching six modems to a simple wooden shelf which were then connected to six phone lines.

With six lines Tang could take on about 50 customers and he opened for business charging each customer £10 a month for internet access. As more people signed up he added more phone lines, but by 1996 his company, Zen Internet, was having to invest so much in new equipment it came close to running out of money. Tang was forced to save the company by borrowing from his family and friends.

Right from the start one of his biggest headaches was that one day a rival company would decide to give away internet access for free and force his company out of business. So when the high street retailer Dixons launched their Freeserve internet service provider in 1998 he feared the worst.

However, while his company did quickly lose most of its personal home users, Tang also discovered to his relief that his business customers were happy to pay for a service that came with customer support. Indeed, the following year Zen Internet made its best ever profit.

Two years later the company faced another challenge with the arrival of broadband. It was a costly gamble but after much agonising Tang decided to take the plunge and upgrade to broadband access. Tang says: 'At the time broadband was very new and was very high risk – and it didn't particularly work that well. It cost us an initial investment of £100,000 which at the time was a hell of a lot of money. But I figured that if we didn't change to broadband then we would get left behind.'

It was a smart decision – Zen Internet now has almost 60,000 customers, of which 43,000 take its broadband service. Tang says: 'Investing in broadband meant that we went from being quite a small regional internet service provider to being a national ISP, and that is what has really driven our success since then.' Zen Internet's sales have doubled every year since the company began and are set to be £40 million in 2006, producing a profit of £3.2 million.

Tang, now 40, still owns 100 per cent of the company, which is now worth around £15 million. He thinks the secret of his success is determination. 'I can focus on something to the point of being obsessive. In the early days I worked seven days a week, 12 hours a day. I did nothing other than work eat and sleep.'

He thinks that the secret of choosing a winning idea is timing. He says: 'It has to be something which is small and has a definite niche in the market but which has potential to grow. Look for something that is just starting out where there is not much happening at the moment. A good example is video on demand through the internet – people talk about it a lot but hardly anyone actually watches movies through the internet. Timing is very important. It is much more difficult to get into a mature market.'

You also need luck. He says: 'Although Dan and I could see back in 1995 that the internet had potential, we had no idea just how much it would develop over the next 10 years. I don't think anybody did. We were very lucky to pick an idea which has grown so much – because despite there being much bigger players than us in the market, it was growing so fast that there was enough business for everybody. Whereas if someone had an idea to start up an internet service provider now, unless they had got significant funding they would have no chance.'

Tang says his brother has no regrets about deciding not to be part of the company. He says: 'He has no interest in business at all.' However, Tang has been keen to ensure that Daniel benefits from the success of the business so for the past few years Zen Internet has funded Daniel's continuing research into artificial intelligence. Tang has also offered to pay to put together a team of researchers to help his brother speed up his research. Daniel also occasionally works for the company as a break from the intensity of his research, recently even spending several months there as head chef.

As for Tang, he is immensely proud of what he has achieved. 'I am absolutely over the moon. It is such a good feeling to have built this up and to have created an environment where people working for the company are enthused by it. I have no interest in selling the business because I don't just aspire to having a big bank balance. I created this business from scratch and I want to see just how far it can go.'

21

Carole Nash

Founder of Carole Nash
Insurance Consultants

Carole Nash's father always hoped she would become a doctor. But Nash was far more interested in sport than academic pursuits as a child. She says: 'I was the tennis captain and the hockey captain and I was so proud of my badges on my tie.'

So at 18 Nash left school to work in an insurance company not far from where she lived in Manchester. She says: 'My father had a lot more ambition for me than I had. But I knew my limitations.'

She joined the firm as a junior in the motor insurance department and quickly discovered she liked the insurance world. 'I loved the contact with the public on the phone. I really got a buzz about it. It was far better than having my head in a book studying physics.'

She also met her future husband in the firm, where he was the superintendent of the claims department. They got married and moved to work in the company's head office in London for three years before returning to

Manchester to raise a family. Nash gave up work at the age of 27 and spent the next 12 years at home looking after their two children.

But one day in 1981, at the age of 39, Nash spotted an advert in the local paper put there by an insurance company that was looking for someone to help out for three hours a day. She took the job, thinking that the money would help pay school fees. The firm quickly realised that Nash had more experience than most of their staff and put her in charge of the motorcycle section.

She says: 'In the beginning I didn't want to be involved with bikes, I thought it was a distasteful idea.' But she took over running the section and soon discovered she actually quite enjoyed it. Nash employed several part-time staff to help her and, remembering her own experiences as a working mother, introduced flexible working for her staff.

She says: 'When I went back to work I knew how stressful it could be if your children were not well. So if someone had a child who was ill I used to tell them they could come in and work in the evening instead.'

Then in 1985 the insurance company decided to shut their northern office and pull out of motorcycle insurance because they felt it was a loss earner. It was then that Nash had her big idea. She knew that one of the policies the firm offered had never had a claim made against it. It was a tiny policy designed specifically for vintage motorcycles and although it did not generate a lot of income she decided to try to keep the policy going herself. 'It was a brilliant policy and it was the only one available on the market which suited the requirements of vintage motorcycle owners. The insurance company were just going to get rid of it and so I felt I was the saviour of it.'

Her former employers agreed to let her take the scheme on, provided that she did so on an independent basis. So, with redundancy money of £2,300, Nash bought professional indemnity and had a separate phone line installed in the dining room of the family home so that she could use that room as her office. She says: 'I had £100 left over so I brought some pens and biros and a book for my phone calls.'

Then she sat at the dining room table and waited for the phone to ring. 'At first it was a little bit rocky because when policyholders realise that something is different, they are

Fact file

Date of birth: 18 December 1941

Marital status: married with two children

Qualifications: one A level

Interests: watching Manchester City play football, swimming, cooking

Personal philosophy: 'If you look after the pence the pounds will look after themselves.'

always a little bit apprehensive. But I was a sunny voice on the end of the phone assuring them that everything was fine.'

Soon other motorbike clubs wanted to join the scheme and by the end of her first year in business Nash had taken £30,000 in premium income.

Her business started to grow by word of mouth and soon she was invited to vintage motorcycle events to publicise her scheme. The first one was the Banbury Run in Oxfordshire. She says: 'I arrived with my proposal forms in a plastic carrier bag and they gave me a little garden table and a stool to sit on.'

Nash also began attending biker club nights in pubs to tell them about her policies.

She says: 'People didn't understand what they were paying for so I used to tell them what they got for their policy and the difference between comprehensive and third party fire and theft.'

As her business grew she moved her office into the garage and got her son Malcolm to help her. But when bikers started coming round to pay their premiums in person she decided it was time to move into a proper office of her own.

After five years Nash's premium income had risen to £1 million and Nash and her husband were attending motorbike events every weekend all over Europe. It was not long before she started buying vintage motorbikes of her own to take to events.

She says: 'Our working day didn't finish at half past five on a Friday night and it started again on Saturday and Sunday when we were off to events. And if we didn't go with a bike we bought a caravan so we would be there at the event and offer our policyholders tea or coffee. Bikers would ring me up to find out if I was going to an event and when I said yes they would say: 'In that case I'll come and pay my renewal, it will save me a stamp.''

Nash now has eight vintage motorbikes including a 1914 BSA Combination, two Morgan three-wheelers and a 1925 Model T Triumph. She says: 'People think a business is driven by the hobby but mine was the other way round. I just loved talking to people at motorbike events and it was just the whole camaraderie that sparked it off.'

Her enthusiasm has been good for business too. She says: 'It really helped to promote the business because we were going to events alongside our policyholders. So if any policyholders had got a comment which was good or bad about our policies, we would pick it up personally.'

In recognition of her involvement, in 1994 she became the first woman to become president of the Vintage Motorcycle Club.

As the business grew Nash started offering insurance policies for modern motorbikes. She also opened an office in Southern Ireland after realising that vintage motorcyclists there had no insurance policies to fit their needs. She says: 'Their hobby was going to die because they had no insurance that fitted the requirements of the vintage motorcyclist. So when the single market came in I dragged my son to the European Parliament to see the people who were in charge of the insurance side of it. They told us to just go out and do it.'

Nash also expanded into offering policies for classic cars, then modern cars, and then travel and household insurance. By 1996 she decided that she needed more professional help running the business and brought in a managing director.

She also opened a body workshop to repair bikes and now has garages around the country which have been approved by the company to carry out repairs.

In 2006 Carole Nash Insurance Consultants is expected to have revenues of £85 million, including £59 million of premium income from policies.

Nevertheless Nash, who owns 51 per cent of the company, says she is not motivated by making money. 'The bottom line is excellent but it was getting to that bottom line that I enjoyed. Some people put too much pressure on making money and wanting to run before they can walk. I was the opposite. I did it because I loved it. Looking back at the fun I have had from of all this, it is like a fairy story.'

She thinks one of the secrets of her success has been to take her time over making big decisions. She says: 'I think about things for a long time and I look at it from the other person's point of view. I put myself in their position and think about why they are saying this or doing that. I analyse the whole situation. If anybody comes up to me with an idea I don't say "Oh, that's a good idea" straightaway, I go away and think about it, even if it's when I am cooking dinner.'

She adds: 'I am a perfectionist. If something is done, it has got to be done right. If I send a letter out to somebody I never send the first one out, I always have to think about it and play around with it.'

22

Spencer Swaffer
Founder of Spencer Swaffer Antiques

Every Friday morning for the past 20 years without fail Spencer Swaffer has made sure he is the first person to enter Paris's famous Porte de Clignancourt fleamarket when it opens. Swaffer, now 55, says: I am very superstitious and I have to be the first person through the gates. It used to open at 4 o'clock in the morning but now it happens at 6 am so I get a bit of a lie-in.' Indeed, he has become such a familiar face that the dealers there have nicknamed him Fleaman and L'Inevitable, because it is inevitable that he will be there.

Brought up near Brighton, Swaffer was an only child and from the age of 10 spent his spare time roaming the South Downs looking for shards of Roman pottery and Neolithic axe heads. As his collection grew he started his own museum in his bedroom, charging visitors twopence a time to see his collection of fossils, Roman pottery and birds' eggs, which he added to with items he found at jumble sales. He says: 'I would buy anything wacky or quirky. My parents were very enthusiastic about it, and they always encouraged me.'

As word of his museum spread, at the age of 12 Swaffer was interviewed by the *Today* programme on Radio 4. Soon afterwards an antiques dealer came to visit his museum and after paying his twopence entry fee, offered Swaffer £50 for some Egyptian Scarab beetle beads that the boy had bought in a jumble sale for a penny.

It was a defining moment. Swaffer says: 'I suddenly discovered I rather preferred making money to being a curator of a museum. So I closed the museum and threw the birds' nests away.'

Swaffer started taking stalls in local antiques markets, and despite his youth made sure he at least looked the part by always wearing a shirt and tie. He learnt what to buy and sell by watching what other dealers did and by the age of 15 he and a friend who shared his passion were going up to London every weekend to sell antiques in Camden Passage market.

He left school at 18 to open an antiques shop in Brighton, funding it himself with the money he had made at markets.

He says: 'I really loved it. I was always in there at half past seven in the morning and I would still be in there at half past seven at night.'

However, in 1974, when Swaffer was 23, his life was turned upside down. His mother suddenly died of cancer and less than two weeks later his father killed himself because he couldn't live without her.

Swaffer inherited the family bungalow and sold it to buy an old greengrocer's shop in Arundel, West Sussex, which he turned into an antiques shop. He says: 'I called the shop "Ancient and Modern" which I thought was terribly clever but now it really makes me cringe.'

It was at this point that Swaffer stumbled upon his big idea. He decided that instead of stocking his shop with fusty traditional antiques like every other antique shop did, he would take his cue from fashion magazines. He started out by specialising in selling unusual items such as enamel advertising signs which were much in demand by bistros at the time. Then when the English country house look came into fashion Swaffer stocked his shop with oak dressers and squishy armchairs. And when that was followed by a desire for French furniture, he stocked that instead. He says: 'Everyone wanted French – everything had to be twiddly and have little carved ribbons and cherubs and carved baskets of flowers and angels.'

Fact file

Date of birth: 28 January 1951

Marital status: married three times with three children

Qualifications: five O levels and two A levels

Interests: reading

Personal philosophy: 'You can only concentrate on one thing at a time.'

Soon Swaffer was driving 3,000 miles each week to buy from dealers and auctions across the country. The shop did so well that after three years Swaffer had run out of space and had to move to bigger premises close by.

His buying sprees did not always go smoothly, however. He once bought a pickled egg jar from a Chinese takeaway and within minutes realised that the van was crawling with lice.

Another time he bought a wooden case containing a life-sized plaster model of a human body. 'I tied it to the roof rack but halfway up the M1 the lid of the box blew off and all the organs went flying down the motorway. People must have thought there had been a horrendous accident.'

Then in 2000 the flat above the shop caught fire. Swaffer and his staff had just two hours to get all his antiques out before the roof collapsed and the fireman turned on their hoses. Fortunately everything was saved and the following day he continued to do business from under the apple tree in the garden.

Another threat to his business came in 2001 with the collapse of the US stock market and the events of September 11th. He says: 'On September 10th our appointments board was full of meetings arranged with American dealers every day for the next month. Within 24 hours of the disaster the board was completely wiped clean.'

Fortunately, Swaffer was able to find a market for his antiques among English private buyers until the US market recovered. His business is expected to have sales of £4 million in 2006.

He has also had to overcome difficulties in his own life. One morning in 2005 Swaffer woke up to discover that overnight he had gone blind in one eye. It was because of a retinal vein thrombosis and his sight in that eye will never return. He says: 'I took it very badly. For the first two or three months after it happened I was unbearable because I was so scared and so upset. The most difficult thing to cope with is the fear of losing the other eye.'

The loss of one eye put a temporary end for a few months to Swaffer's buying trips to France but fortunately it did not put an end to his ability to buy antiques. Swaffer quickly discovered that because he had bought from them for many years the French dealers were happy to e-mail pictures to him of antiques they thought he might be interested in. Indeed, he would often come into the shop in a morning and discover 40 pictures waiting for him to choose from.

Swaffer thinks that his early idea of following fashion trends has been key to the business's success.

He says: 'I think I have withstood the peaks and troughs of the market because I am in the fashion business, not in the antiques business. And that means no brown sideboards. Most English antiques dealers are interested in antiques in a rather academic way. They tend to be very stuck in their ways and sell the same boring things. But I have always been an avid reader of magazines because they are terribly influential on what young people want.'

He adds: 'An antiques dealer at an auction will walk round a piece of furniture, they will turn it upside down, they will get a torch out and a magnifying glass and then they will go and look at their reference books. But I'll view it in five seconds.'

He is also proud of the fact that he has always managed to keep the business debt-free. 'Because I don't owe any money, I am quite prepared to take a loss on something if it has been here for a while. And if I pay £2,000 for something I am very happy to sell it for £2,200.'

Now 55 and married to his third wife, he says: 'I am colossally proud of what I have achieved, to the point of conceit. And I don't care who knows it.'

He admits though that he is driven by the fear that it could all end tomorrow. 'I am driven by a fear of failure and by the desire to be the best at what I do. If a cheque doesn't arrive I can feel physically ill.'

Despite the loss of his eye Swaffer has no plans to retire and says that even after more than 40 years in the antiques business, he never tires of it. He still does all the buying for the shop himself and never like to goes away for more than five days' holiday at a time. He says: 'For me it is all about the thrill of the hunt.'

Ideally he would even like to be buried in the shop's garden when the time comes, although he says: 'I am having a bit of trouble getting my wife to agree because she is worried about the resale value.'

23

Helen Colley
Founder of Farmhouse Fare

Between the ages of 5 and 16 Helen Colley was bullied at school. 'I was freckled and dumpy, and I tended to be introverted. I threw myself into my studies but then I had to wear glasses and the bullying got worse. Even now I think my perception of myself is different because of that,' she says.

Because of the bullying, her home life became increasingly important to her. Born and brought up with two brothers on her parents' dairy farm in Lancashire, Colley spent much of her time thinking up things to do. At the age of 9 she made animals out of shells and sold them in post offices, and at the age of 14 she set up a tearoom in the front room of the house.

She says: 'I used to enter loads of cookery and craft competitions and I would enter gymkhanas with my pony. I have always been quite competitive. I competed with myself more than anyone else.'

Colley also learnt the value of hard work. She says: 'We all had to go out and work on the farm. It would be all hands on deck. I did the hens and the calves. I also enjoyed baking and would help mum with the cooking.'

From the age of 10 Colley started working in local restaurants and cafes. When she left school she wanted to go to catering college but because she could already cook she was sent on a two-year hotel management course instead.

While on the course she started working as a cleaner and waitress at a stately home called Gisburn Park, where shooting parties were held. It was an eye opening experience.

She says: 'At one of these shooting parties a woman called Lavinia came to cook and she made a pudding called chocolate roulade. Back then puddings were fruit flans and trifles, and I thought, wow, that is what I want to do. I want to cook wonderful meals for people. I can be the Lancashire version of Lavinia.'

Just before she graduated from college, however, she became ill with a virus for a few months and missed the final exam. Even though she was the best student in her class, the college said she would have to take the whole two-year course again. She refused and left.

Without a qualification however Colley could not get a job and so she decided to start her own business as a caterer. A bank agreed to give her a £250 overdraft facility and her parents let her use their kitchen.

Colley says: 'They had a huge farmhouse kitchen and they let me put in a hand basin and pull up the carpet. I got the environmental health officer out and he told me what to do. Then I got 1,000 flyers printed saying I was going to do freezer meals and small parties and got my brothers to hand out the leaflets locally.'

At first Colley got work doing teas for a friend's parents who ran a funeral business. She also made pies and bread to sell in post offices and local shops, getting up at 3 am to make bread.

As word spread she started catering for weddings and parties in marquees throughout the north of England.

Her business expanded and she moved into unused farm buildings on her parents' land and converted them into kitchens. Then one day in 2001 she held a coffee morning for charity and invited all her catering clients. To raise more money for the charity she also made some sticky toffee puddings to sell. They were a huge success.

Fact file

Date of birth: 29 March 1966

Marital status: married with three children

Qualifications: none

Interests: ballroom dancing, organising the village duck race, walking the dog

Personal philosophy: 'Have no regrets. The worst thing for me is not to try doing something.'

She says: 'Everyone loved them. They sold out straight-away and people started asking me why they couldn't buy them anywhere.'

It was then Colley had her big idea. She decided to start making sticky toffee puddings to sell in local delicatessens and butchers' shops. By now married with three children, she somewhat optimistically thought that making puddings would give her the chance to take life a little easier.

'I had spent 18 years working every night and every weekend and having no time off and I wanted to have more time to see my children. I even had very short hair because it was easier to wash, and I wore army boots all the time because I was constantly jumping out into fields. I thought maybe there was a different way of doing things', she says.

As well as sticky toffee puddings she began to make other traditional ones such as bread and butter pudding, using recipes her mother taught her as a child and always using natural ingredients that people would find in their store cupboard at home.

Her puddings sold so well in local shops that Booths, the supermarket chain, agreed to stock them as well. Within months Sainsbury's heard about her puddings and called to say they wanted to stock Colley's sticky toffee puddings in its northern stores.

Her decision to start making puddings could not have been timed better. Just a few weeks after she started supplying Sainsbury's, in the summer of 2002, foot-and-mouth disease hit the countryside. It forced the closure of many farms and demand for her outside catering and marquee events completely dried up.

It was however a miserable way to be proved right. Her parents' prized pedigree Holstein herd had to be destroyed by the army and their farm was closed down. 'It was a horrendous time', she says. 'My parents had spent 40 years breeding their herd and it was suddenly wiped out.'

Faced with a family crisis Colley was determined not to let her business suffer too. She promptly created a separate entrance to the farm for her business and focused all her energies on making puddings.

She says: 'I am a great believer in fate. I think things happen for a reason and you have got to grab the opportunity and go with it. I thought I can either sit here and watch my business crumble around me or I can pull myself together and do something about it.'

The army moved onto the farm to shut down her business but she refused to let them. She says: 'We had to go through barricades to get to work.'

With no herd to look after, her father started delivering the puddings around the country in a van. Colley says: 'I think that the puddings actually kept our sanity on the farm because it gave everybody a focus and a sense of purpose.'

Six months later she sold her outside catering business for just £6,000.

Creating a pudding business was, however, a steep learning curve. She says: 'I found that people don't take your calls so I learnt to become a persistent caller and convince everyone they needed to speak to me. I would call secretaries and become friends with them and eventually they would take pity on me and get the right person to call me back.'

As the pudding business grew Colley continued to use her parents' farm as business premises, but soon she was making so many puddings she had to organise a night shift of packers to meet demand. It was at this point that her father politely suggested it might be time for her to leave home and get a place of her own.

She says: 'I was absolutely gutted. It was like leaving *The Waltons*.'

Colley found an industrial unit close by and spent £150,000 converting it, borrowing the money from her bank and friends and family. The landlord of the premises, also a friend, took a 15 per cent stake in the business and Colley also found a business adviser who eventually became her financial director.

Her company, Farmhouse Fare, now makes 45 different types of pudding and her wares are sold in all leading super-markets. Turnover in 2006 is expected to be £8 million, up from £5 million last year. Now 40, Colley thinks the secret of her success is passion and commitment.

'I love what I do. And I am a determined little thing. There is no stopping me', she says.

'Even if something goes wrong I get back up and dust myself off and start all over again. I think being bullied as a child makes you a strong individual because you realise you have to stand up for yourself.'

Her advice to anyone dreaming of taking the plunge is simple. She says: 'Never live your life on "if only". Too many people make excuses – just do it. At least, if you fail, then you know you have tried.'

24

Don Lewin
Founder of Clinton Cards

At the age of 40 Lewin achieved his lifetime's ambition when he bought himself a brand new Rolls Royce. He had to go up to Manchester to collect it and pay an extra £2,000 to take delivery straightaway because there was a waiting list. But it was worth it. He says: 'It was a great day. Ever since I was a child my ultimate ambition was to own a Rolls Royce. I felt I had arrived.'

There was just one problem. Having achieved his lifetime's ambition, Lewin needed a new goal. So he quickly set himself the target of making an enormous amount of money to keep him focused. He says: 'You do need a goal.'

Lewin was born in the East End of London. His father was the local chimney sweep. From the age of 10 Lewin worked in the markets to make pocket money, selling lead soldiers from a sack on Saturdays and selling dogs bred by a neighbour on Sundays. He says: 'My father never gave me any money, he used to say that if I wanted any money I had to go and earn it.'

Lewin grew up during the Blitz. His school was often bombed and he was evacuated, so his education was patchy.

He left school at 15 to get a job with a building firm and at the age of 18 did two years of National Service before getting a job selling household brushes from door to door.

Lewin moved on to become a tallyman selling credit and then, at the age of 26, he got a job selling greetings cards from the boot of his car to local sweetshops and newsagents. As he built up sales he took on a couple of people to help him. He also bought the lease on a launderette to run as a sideline.

When Lewin had been selling cards for a few years, however, he decided that the retailers were missing a golden opportunity to make money. He says: 'The small newsagents and sweetshops I sold to would put the cards in a drawer and were afraid to buy too many cards in case they did not sell them by Christmas. They were keen to be out of cards by the time Christmas came and happy if they sold out two weeks before. But it occurred to me that if somebody opened a shop which only sold cards then it should work, because I thought that the last two weeks before Christmas could be a busy time for selling cards.'

Friends and other retailers however thought differently. Lewin says: 'They thought I was crackers and thought I would last six months. They didn't think you could make a business work by just selling cards.'

He liked the idea of running a shop for other reasons. He says: 'One of the big things that interested me when I was selling the cards from the back of my car was that if I wanted to have a holiday then my income stopped. But with a shop at least something is going on while you are away. What I liked about cards is that it is somebody's birthday every day so there is something going on all the time.'

So, undaunted, Lewin opened his first shop in Essex in 1968 at the age of 35, calling it Clinton Cards after his six-year-old son. He funded the start-up costs with savings and a bank loan and by persuading two big card firms to provide him with frozen credit. This meant he would only pay them for the cards that he actually sold. He would pay for any cards which were left over when he eventually sold them the following Christmas.

His hunch paid off. He says: 'Everyone's mouths dropped open when they saw what could be sold. People

Fact file

Date of birth: 11 June 1933

Marital status: married with two children

Qualifications: none

Interests: swimming, classic cars

Personal philosophy: 'I have been poor and I have been rich and rich is far better.'

bought Christmas cards right up to Christmas Eve. At the time big boxed cards were fashionable and the amount we sold of them on Christmas Eve was incredible. Men would go to the pub after work and get drunk and then come into our shop where they would buy a card for the wife. And often they would get one for the girlfriend too. It was quite a revelation.'

Within six months the shop was doing so well that Lewin opened a second shop, and then another. He lined the walls with cards and made sure that there was enough space for customers to move around.

He says: 'When I was selling Father's Day cards from the back of my car, I would be lucky to sell six dozen to a shop because retailers felt that Father's Day was a bit chancy for cards. But in my shop I would put ten feet of Father's Day cards on display and sell them.'

When Lewin had amassed a chain of seven shops he decided to sell five of them and reinvest the money in opening larger shops in better locations. This time round he found banks far more willing to lend him money. He also decided to take the lead and create new card-giving occasions. Fifteen years ago he asked the manufacturers to make him some divorce cards – in both congratulations and commiserations wording. He also came up with several notable captions for cards, such as 'To mum and dad on their wedding day'.

He says: 'We need to be constantly on the lookout in this business. It is a fashion business and to keep in front of everybody else we need to be coming up with all these new ideas all the time.' More recently he has created cards for gay couples.

By 1988 Lewin had created a chain of 87 card shops and decided it was time to get some of the money he had invested out of the company. He toyed with the idea of selling the business outright but as both his son and daughter worked for the company he decided to float it on the stock market instead and retain 50 per cent of the shares.

At flotation the company was valued at £20.3 million. Lewin used the £3 million raised from investors to expand the business by acquiring several rival card shop chains.

Dealing with City investors and financiers was, however, initially a shock. He says: 'To start with I found it very difficult to get some enthusiasm for the company. At least 90 per cent of our customers are women so when you try to talk to men in the City about greetings cards, they all switch off because men only buy about three cards a year – for their wife's birthday, for their anniversary and for Christmas.'

Being a family company has not always worked in his favour either. He says: 'Our record as a public company has been wonderful but because the City sees us as a family business I don't think we get the accolades that we deserve.'

Nevertheless, Clinton Cards is currently expected to have sales of around £492 million, has 800 shops in the UK and Ireland and is valued at £140 million on the stock market.

Lewin, who retains a 33 per cent stake, is chairman of the company, his son Clinton is managing director and his daughter Debbie is marketing director. He says: 'I think I am extremely fortunate that I have got two children who are as passionate about the business as I am.'

He admits he has always been ambitious to succeed. He says: 'I always wanted to be a millionaire. I can remember being 22 and feeling that the world was passing me by and that I was never going to make it. When I was ambitious I could taste it, it was that strong. But I never gave up, I just kept working hard. I was prepared to work every hour there was.'

The rewards have been worth it. Now 73, and with several Rolls Royces and Bentleys in his garage, Lewin says: 'Making the first £100 and then the first £1,000 was a long, hard, tedious slog. But the time and the effort and the work were worth it in the end. I have been poor and I have been rich and rich is better, there is no question about that. I enjoy my money. I can have anything I want now, and it is a great feeling.'

25

Chey Garland
Founder of Garland Call Centres

Chey Garland had to learn responsibility at a young age. Brought up in a working class suburb of Middlesbrough, she was the eldest child by some years and so had to look after her younger brother and sister while her parents were out at work. Her father sold fruit and vegetables and her mother worked as a waitress.

Life was hard in other ways, too. 'Mum and Dad didn't have the happiest of marriages,' she says. 'It was quite turbulent. They didn't get on and it wasn't a particularly happy household.'

Garland left school aged 16 with dreams of becoming a receptionist and got a job as an office junior in a roofing company. She soon became interested in the way the business worked and started harbouring secret dreams of becoming managing director. But she also noticed that the only women who progressed through the company's ranks were well educated and from middle class families. 'I could see that working for other people would never fulfil my fantasy of becoming managing director of a company,' she

says. 'I realised I would only attain that by setting up my own business.'

She spent five years working her way round the different departments of the company and found that she was particularly good at collecting debts from late-paying customers. So she got a job as a credit controller with another company and, at the age of 23 and with £600 of savings, she decided to set up her own debt-collection business. She asked several local companies if they might be interested in such a service and then rented the attic of a Victorian house for £5 a week to use as her office.

At this point, though, she still had no actual clients and so asked her local business club if she could speak at one of its monthly meetings about her company. It was the perfect way to find customers. She says: 'I would take as many speaking engagements as I could and I found that, once I had started to build a client base, customers would recommend me to new ones.'

The business expanded from the attic to take over the whole house and in 1984, after three years in business, Garland had amassed enough money to buy a plot of land in Middlesbrough. She also started up a recruitment agency which specialised in placing project engineers and credit management specialists with firms in the oil industry. It did well and after a few years she sold it for a tidy sum.

Meanwhile she built an office block for her credit-management company. By 1993 she had 60 staff and was making a nice profit. But the market was becoming crowded. 'I had reached a size where it was hard to see how I could grow the business any more,' she says.

It was then that Garland had her big idea. She decided that the solution lay in persuading her customers to let her handle all their credit-control operations rather than simply their bad debts. That way she would control the whole activity, dealing with incoming as well as outgoing calls. When one of her clients was taken over by a mobile phone company, a much bigger firm, Garland spotted her opportunity. The larger company had intended to deal with all the additional customer service calls itself in-house, but Garland had other ideas.

She says: 'The company's customer contact centres were located in affluent areas like Cheltenham and Banbury. From

Fact file

Date of birth: 3 March 1957

Marital status: married with two children

Qualifications: none

Interests: restoring her 18th-century walled garden, spending time with her children

Personal philosophy: 'There is more than one way to skin a cat.'

listening to the new management team I realised that because there was a very low unemployment in those areas, the company was struggling to get access to the people they needed to employ. And that even if they did get access to them, the centres would be very expensive to operate.'

Garland was desperate not to lose the business her company already had from the firm that was being taken over. So she sat down and started thinking.

'I kept desperately trying to find a way through this because I felt that there was a different way to tackle it. Ultimately the penny dropped – my call centres were based in the North East where there was very high unemployment and so the cost of operating them was less. I had a pool of great people who are well educated, I had got the space, and so I could be very cost effective.'

Excited by her idea she asked for a meeting with the customer services director and managed to persuade him to let her firm handle their overflow customer services calls for a trial period of 12 weeks. The additional work load would mean Garland taking on 20 extra staff.

She says: 'When she said yes that was one of the sweetest moments. I came out of their office feeling so excited. I got in the car and I told my driver to get out of the car park quickly, because I wanted to act really nonchalant but actually my heart was bursting. Then I got out of the car and I shouted: "Yes!"'

Others, however, did not share her elation. She says: 'When I rang my office I was just met with total apathy. My finance director was like: "Oh yeah, right."'

Undaunted, Garland got to work. The contract was for only 12 weeks but she was convinced that if she did it well, it could be the start of greater things. So she decided that instead of simply incorporating it into her existing business she would invest in new technology and dedicated premises – despite the fact that it would be impossible to pay off the investment it needed in such a short time.

She says: 'I was absolutely convinced that this had legs. I thought that if I got this I could develop it and grow it. My brain started to whirr.'

Once again however, not everyone was convinced. 'Our external accountants lectured me and said: "What the hell are you doing taking your eye off the ball, you have got a good little business there"', she says. 'They wondered why I was bothering with this for a 12-week period. But when you have got to go, you have got to go. They told me not to do it, but I didn't heed their advice.'

Happily, following her instincts paid off. After the trial period the mobile phone company extended the contract for another three months and Garland got more work with another arm of the company.

But then things took a bad turn. Garland learnt that the mobile phone company was planning to outsource an important contract to a call centre – but had not asked Garland to bid for the work because it thought that her company was too small. She says: 'I felt as though I had had my heart and lungs ripped out.'

She refused to bow out without a fight. She demanded to be given the right to bid, turned down work from other companies in order to focus on it, and even took on new premises to prove she was capable of handling the contract. Once again, her determination paid off. She was awarded the contract three days before Christmas and it transformed the company. Garland Call Centres now employs 2,900 staff and in 2006 sales are expected to be £47 million. Its clients include Virgin, Vodafone and Sky.

Now 49, Garland says that all of her business ideas have grown out of something she is already involved in. 'My ideas tend to develop out of something I am doing. It is like selling baked beans and then thinking, well actually, tinned spaghetti might be a good idea as well. And come to think of it, why don't we do some rice pudding as well.'

Garland, who still owns the whole company, admits she is driven by the desire to prove herself. 'As a child I never really felt that I was noticed,' she says. 'I never felt that I achieved anything or that there was any expectation of me to achieve anything. So proving myself is something that is important to me and so is establishing respect for what I have achieved.'

She says she still has a lot more to achieve. 'I don't feel completed or finished,' she says. 'I think that everyone has a finest hour and I don't think I have had mine yet. I feel like I am climbing loads of hills – as I get to the top of the hill I look over and there seem to be loads more hills to climb.'

26

Andy Thornton
Founder of Andy Thornton Ltd

Andy Thornton had an unconventional upbringing. Throughout his childhood he and his family lived in a trolleybus. He says: 'It was difficult to get building materials after the war and my father refused to borrow money. So he bought an old single-decker trolleybus and put on a wooden extension. It was very cosy.' Even when the family moved to a farm with outbuildings in Lincolnshire, his father simply dismantled the trolleybus and moved it with them.

For Thornton it was the perfect childhood. From the age of six he loved making things from wood and as he grew older he would use the outbuildings as a workshop. At grammar school he was made to study Latin instead of woodwork because he was in one of the top streams. But he persuaded the woodwork teacher to let him stay in every lunchtime for three years so he could keep on doing woodwork as well.

Thornton went to Loughborough University to do a degree in education with the aim of becoming a woodwork teacher. But first, after qualifying, he decided to spend four years travelling the world with his girlfriend, Kate.

They started in the United States, where Thornton worked as a joiner and carpenter. In Philadelphia he got a job restoring architectural salvage and met the man who would change his life. John Wilson ran an architectural antiques store in California and offered Thornton a job.

Thornton says: 'He would fly me out to the East Coast where I would dismantle an interior of a building, load it into a truck and drive it back across to the West Coast.'

After six months, Thornton and Kate were keen to resume travelling but Wilson did not have enough money to pay him his wages so he agreed to stay on and run an auction sale to raise the cash.

The auction was a big success as US pub and restaurant owners snapped up the salvage to refit their interiors in a traditional style. The couple resumed their travels, but over the next couple of years regularly flew back to California to run more auction sales for Wilson.

By the time Thornton and Kate – now his wife after a spur-of-the-moment marriage in Las Vegas – returned to Britain in 1975, they had amassed savings of £4,000. It was then that Thornton had his big idea. He decided to take part in the next auction himself. He invested the entire sum buying architectural salvage such as doors, panelling and stained glass windows rescued from buildings that were being demolished.

He says: 'I kept the stuff in a little semi-derelict building and when Kate's mother came down and saw all this stock she just burst into tears because it looked like junk. She was absolutely devastated and said I had had enough money to put down a deposit on a semi-detached house.'

Thornton's conviction nevertheless paid off. He shipped his salvage to the auction in the United States and trebled his money.

He started sending containers of architectural salvage to the auction each year, racing to industrial Victorian buildings earmarked for demolition around the North of England to rescue interiors before the demolition workers got there.

He says: 'At that time you could buy stuff very cheaply – the race was to get there before the demolition men destroyed it and burned it. We got iron railings, interiors of

Fact file

Date of birth: 28 May 1949

Marital status: married with two children

Qualifications: BA in education from Nottingham University

Interests: hiking, sailing, tennis, collecting antiques

Personal philosophy: 'Do whatever it takes. And try and be fair with people.'

pubs, banks, chemist shops, churches. The demolition men thought I was a crank because I would pay them for all this woodwork and take it out myself which would save them the hassle of stripping it out and burning it.'

One time he paid a demolition company for a bandstand, which they were already being paid to demolish by the council, and dismantled it himself. It ended up becoming a golf club house in Kansas.

He says: 'Sometimes I used to feel a bit guilty exporting this stuff to America but there was just no demand for it in England. It was out of fashion and nobody wanted it.'

As traditional English pub interiors became less easily available Thornton hired craftsmen to turn decorative woodwork from churches and other buildings into bar fittings.

He continued to send salvage to Wilson's auctions every year and at the 1979 auction Thornton made so much profit that he decided to get a bank loan and build a 10,000 square foot factory in West Yorkshire for £130,000.

But then disaster struck. Confident of another success, Thornton sent a large shipment of salvage to be sold at auction. However the market had turned sour. Thornton says: 'The sale was a three-day nightmare. Interest rates were high and the hospitality industry, which usually bought old bars and restaurant interiors at the sale, wasn't prepared to borrow money at that rate. Stuff got sold off cheaply because there were no reserve prices. It was horrendous. Break-even was US $12 million and the auction actually grossed US $7 million – there was a US $5 million shortfall.'

Wilson was wiped out, and Thornton himself lost about £220,000.

He says: 'I was supposed to come back to pay the bank off with the proceeds of the auction and couldn't. I had 24 employees, a brand new factory and a lot of debt. I was worried sick.' The timing could not have been worse as Kate was pregnant with their second child.

Thornton cut the staff to eight and started trying to find new markets for his salvage. 'The factory was a millstone round our neck. I got a stomach ulcer for a while. The dilemma was what to do with all this stock. I was renting a big old woollen mill which was full of all this salvage and I had to convert it into cash to survive.'

He adds: 'The worst part was not knowing what to do because I didn't have a direction. I knew that no matter how hard the eight of us worked in the factory, I couldn't pay the overheads.'

At one point their accountant even recommended closing down the business and renting out the factory. After much agonising Thornton decided that the only way out of the mess was to grow the business.

He says: 'I had used the deeds of our house as collateral for the factory, so Kate and I lived like church mice and worked like hell.'

At the last minute Thornton decided to take a stand at an interior design exhibition in London and discovered that breweries in this country were now looking for salvaged interiors to refit their pubs. He fitted out a hotel in Wales, and then he did a restaurant called the Chicago Rib Shack in London. It received a lot of publicity because Princess Diana took her sons there and suddenly Thornton's interiors were back in demand. Soon other pubs and restaurants were asking for his salvage. And when they asked if he could install the interiors for them, he did that too.

He says: 'The brewers were fed up of all the plastic and Formica of the sixties and seventies. Often we were putting pubs back to how they had been.'

He also made a profit selling old pub signs back to their owners. He says: 'I had bought hundreds of these Tetley pub signs when the company was modernising its pubs and had stockpiled them because I had too many to sell at one go. So pubs would phone me up and say: "Have you still got the Blue Bull?" Then they would buy it back again.'

As genuine pub interiors became more scarce, he also started importing reproduction fittings, stained glass and furniture from the United States to sell to pubs and restaurants here.

Then in 1983 Thornton brought in two shareholders, one taking 10 per cent and the other 5 per cent. The company also began exporting its salvage and reproduction products overseas, and today it designs and builds interiors around the world.

Happily, Thornton's dogged persistence has paid off. The company now has 180 employees and is expected to have a turnover of £15 million in 2006. In November 2005 Thornton sold the company to his management team for a substantial undisclosed sum. He plans to use his free time to do more travelling.

Thornton, now 57, says that dealing with the bad times was a huge learning curve. 'Prior to the disastrous auction all I could ever see was the upside, but afterwards I started looking at what could be the downside. Since then I have run the business much more cautiously because after all the worry of that period I wanted to be able sleep at night. Fear of failure was a huge driving force because I didn't want to let people down.'

Still married to Kate after 31 years and with two children, he thinks that being brought up in a trolleybus played an important role in shaping his character. He says: 'I think it made me more independent-minded. I don't necessarily go with the flow or follow convention.'

27

Nick Austin

Founder of Vivid Imaginations

The first time Nick Austin tried his hand at being an entrepreneur he was just eight years old. He used to sing in the
church choir and every Christmas the choir would go carol
singing around the village to raise money for charity. One
year, however, Austin and a friend decided to go carol
singing alone – and keep all the money for themselves. He
admits now: 'It was a really devious thing to do.'

Brought up in a large middle class family outside
Wolverhampton, Austin failed the 11 plus but eventually
managed to get enough A levels to take a degree in business
studies at Portsmouth Polytechnic. After graduating in 1979
he got a job as a trainee with British Steel.

He hated it. He says: 'There was a steel strike going on so I
had to walk through the picket line every day. I was spat on
and called a scab. It was horrible.'

So in his spare time he started up a small business with
three friends organising tours to Holland and Belgium for
amateur football clubs who wanted to play teams over there.
The business made money but the work was exhausting.

And after 18 months it became clear that the business could not sustain all four partners so Austin and two others dropped out.

He left British Steel to join Proctor & Gamble but soon realised he was not cut out for corporate life. He says: 'I found it too stifling. I was too rebellious and asked awkward questions in meetings.'

He joined a toy company instead and at the age of 29 was given the job of revitalising Matchbox toys, which had just come out of receivership. He and the finance director Alan Bennie managed to make a success of it but when the business was sold Austin decided he wanted to start up a toy company of his own.

He says: 'I was fed up of making money for other people. I had a really juicy offer to join another company but I just couldn't stomach the idea of going back into corporate life. I was thoroughly disenchanted with it and used to feel as though I was working with a straitjacket on.'

He could see that toys were increasingly being based on characters from television shows and films, but that so far the shows and characters they were based on were all American. Austin's big idea was to start making toys based on characters from British shows.

He says: 'I had watched the growth of character licensing – putting a character on a product – and realised that all the big properties always came from America, such as *Star Wars* or *Superman*. I thought there had to be an opportunity to exploit local and European output. I could see that kids were watching more television and more movies, and there were more entertainment characters coming through that you could make toys from. All I had to do was be brave enough to identify the characters which were closer to home.'

His wife Kate, however, took some persuading. He says: 'She didn't want me to go on my own so I promised her that if it didn't work within 18 months then I would go back to corporate life.'

Austin called his company Vivid Imaginations and persuaded his former colleague Alan Bennie to join him. Between them they managed to raise £250,000 by pooling the severance money they received from their old company and remortgaging their homes. Then after much effort they

Fact file

Date of birth: 2 July 1957

Marital status: married with two children

Qualifications: BA (Hons) business studies degree from Portsmouth Polytechnic

Interests: playing tennis and golf, skiing

Personal philosophy: 'Success is 1 per cent inspiration and 99 per cent perspiration.'

found a bank willing to give them a rolling overdraft for the same amount. Austin says: 'Most of the banks laughed deliriously because at that time the British toy industry had a bad reputation as so many companies had gone bust.'

Austin decided that the first toy they made should be an Action-Man style doll based on the 1960s *Captain Scarlet* television series. He was gambling on the fact that as the BBC's re-runs of the *Thunderbird* series had been such a hit with viewers it would decide to give *Captain Scarlet*, the sequel, another airing too. Luckily Austin's gamble paid off. Just three months after they started up their business the BBC put *Captain Scarlet* back on air in a prime time slot and the toys flew off the shelves. Austin's company made £10 million in sales. He says: 'Suddenly in our first year of business *Captain Scarlet* provided us with the number one boys' toy in the market place. It was staggering.'

Their next big success followed soon after – in the shape of dolls modelled on the members of boy band Take That. Austin explains: 'We realised that some of their fans were as young as seven or eight, which was the same age as girls who buy Barbie dolls. So we thought that if we had good lookalike dolls of their heroes then young girls would buy them. Everybody does that now, but at the time it was quite high risk and pioneering.'

Not all of the toys Austin has thought up have been quite as successful, however. Seven years ago his company invested heavily in a new television series called *Space Precinct* in the hope that the BBC would give it a prime time slot on Saturday evenings which would bring in a big audience. But the BBC decided to show it on Monday evenings instead. Austin says: 'The kids didn't know about it, the craze never took off, we sold hardly anything and it was a commercial disaster. We lost about £400,000.'

Then six years ago Austin and his partner Bennie faced a different kind of challenge. They decided to sell the company to a US venture capital company for £27 million, giving Austin a personal fortune of close to £10 million, on the condition that the two of them stayed on to run the company for five years before moving on. He says: 'They offered us a lot of money and we were young and thought this is great, it is our opportunity to cash in.'

But when the five years were almost up the two of them realised that they didn't want to leave after all. So with the help of a British venture capital firm Phoenix Equity Partners they staged a management buy-out and bought Vivid Imaginations back for £62 million, sharing the ownership with employees and retaining 4 per cent each for themselves.

Austin is philosophical about buying back the company for a lot more than he sold it for. He says: 'We suddenly realised that we loved what we were doing. We sometimes laugh about it and say: "Crikey, why did we do that?" But at that particular moment in time it felt like the right thing to do and I think that is the only way you can look at it. There are no big regrets because the business has made many people wealthy and very happy.'

Vivid Imaginations is now Britain's largest toy company with sales of £148 million projected for 2006. Last year one of its leading brands, Bratz, achieved the unthinkable and pushed Barbie off the number one doll slot, which it had held for 45 years.

Austin thinks that much of his desire to succeed comes from some unhappy experiences as a child. He says: 'I was really small as a kid so in sport I always had to try so much harder than everybody else. I was also prone to getting bullied so I had to really stick up for myself. I am sure those tough formative years made me the competitive and driven person that I am. I have always felt that I had something to prove.'

He adds: 'I have never felt that I was a particularly brilliant or creative person. But I also very rarely meet anybody who is more driven than I am. Everything I do, I have to do at 100 miles an hour – and win.'

Now 48, he thinks his achievements are also due to a healthy dose of paranoia. He says: 'Someone once said that only the paranoid survive and I feel as if I have got that burned across the front of my brain. I am driven by a fear of failure. I just can't stand the idea of losing. Our industry is so precarious that unless you are working flat out all the time to come up with hot new toys, the chances are you will go backwards. But once you have got some success behind you the last thing you ever want to do is go backwards. I feel that if we ever take our foot off the pedal then a competitor will come and steal our crown.'

28

Cheryl Grant

Founder of White Label Productions

Having chronic asthma has had a big effect on Cheryl Grant's life. Unable to run around and play with the other children, Grant spent much of her childhood indoors looking at magazines and playing music. She says: 'My mother always had old magazines lying around so I used to pore through those. I was really interested in clothes and fashion and books. And I would listen to my parents' record collection. They had a bit of classical music but it was mainly Cliff Richard.'

She was born and brought up with her younger brother in a council block of flats in Inverness, where her father worked as a printer. She did not enjoy school much. She says: 'I hated it. I can't emphasise that enough. I am not very good at being told what to do. I was more interested in boys and going out. I was always misbehaving.'

At 18 she went to college in Edinburgh to do a degree in publishing and then took a postgraduate degree in marketing. She says: 'I did it so I didn't have to get a proper job. I would be lying if I said anything else.'

On graduating she got a job at Longmans publishing in Edinburgh as an editorial assistant. But she couldn't type and lasted just three months. She then spent a year in Harlow working as a production editor on academic magazines before getting a job with publishing company Emap helping to produce health and baby magazines.

At the age of 25 Grant got a job as a production manager with the record label Decca, then part of Polygram, after spotting an advert for the position in the paper. She spent the next 13 years working her way up the company, ending up as a vice president in charge of the marketing services department which designed and packaged the music the company released. She says: 'I spent a long time there because selling something like music has an emotive connection. It is addictive.'

While she was at Decca she also took an MBA at Thames Valley University. She had always been quite keen on the idea of starting up her own business, once considering the possibility of starting up a venture providing alternative therapies. She says: 'I had a friend who had a chain of alternative therapy clinics and I thought it was a really interesting business. I thought I could manage something like that because often the people who provide the treatments are not particularly good at running a business.'

When she started looking into it, however, she decided not to pursue it. 'It didn't instinctively feel quite right. I enjoyed the creativity of the music industry and so I thought I should stick with what I know. I think you know when it is your time to set up something because the idea that comes to you is one which you really believe in and think you can make work.'

In the event her time came in 2001 when she and the rest of the management team were asked to undertake a major review of the company. Decca, by this time part of Universal, was shifting from selling traditional classical records to selling more mainstream classical 'crossover' music by artists who were promoted like pop acts and so sold in larger quantities. Grant quickly realised that this meant there would be a lot less work for her department.

After discussing the situation with a colleague, the vice president of finance, whom she had worked with for many years, she realised she had a stark choice to make. 'I had one

Fact file

Date of birth: 21 December 1962

Marital status: married with two children

Qualifications: MA in business administration and MBA from Thames Valley University

Interests: aerobics, cooking

Personal philosophy: 'Live for today.'

of two options. I could either hold onto my job and get rid of virtually all my team of 25 people, or I could go out and borrow some money and set up a business of my own with an outsourcing contract from Decca.'

After much agonising she decided to do the latter. She says: 'It took me about six months to decide to do it and numerous plans to try to make the financial dynamics work. But most of my team were excellent and I thought I could sell their services to other clients as well as to Decca. I had worked with many of them for years and I knew they were the best in the business. I felt it was a win–win situation because it meant that Universal would be able to reduce their overheads and yet have the service as and when they needed it.'

In the end it took 18 months to come up with a workable plan which both she and the board of Universal were happy with. One of the hardest things was keeping the news from her staff. She says: 'It was horrible. I couldn't look at anybody I worked with.'

Finally, in 2002, at the age of 39 and with two children under the age of six, Grant was ready to put her plan into action. She remortgaged the family house to raise the £50,000 she needed to set up the company, which she called White Label Productions. Then she immediately re-employed 14 of the 25 people who had previously worked for her at Decca.

Then she got to work trying to win more contracts for her fledgling company, which provided every service from styling artists and taking their pictures to designing their websites, packaging their records and writing press releases.

She says: 'The Decca contract alone wasn't enough so I had to go out and start selling our services. It was quite stressful and I don't suppose I was very nice to live with. But I am an eternal optimist. And at the end of the day it was quite rewarding because if you mess it up then the only person you have got to blame is yourself.'

After more than a year of running the company at a loss Grant managed to secure a contract with EMI. It was a crucial turning point for the business and soon other contracts followed. The company now has 12 clients and is on target to have sales of £4 million in 2006 after looking after the creative side of artists such as Russell Watson, Nigel Kennedy and Andrea Bocelli.

Grant says that turning her former department into a stand-alone business has made her not only more focused on the need to make profits, but also more conscious of the need to be continually creative. She says: 'We try to get as many creative ideas into the business as we can. Working with lots of different clients and labels and artists means you have to stay fresh. We actively go out to see more exhibitions and buy more art books that we used to.'

It has not been entirely stress-free. Once there was a mix-up at the manufacturers and one of their classical DVDs ended up with porn and tag wrestling on it. The mistake was not discovered until the DVD reached the shops.

Nowadays though, the biggest problem she has is artists claiming to be a lot thinner than they really are. 'We do all the styling and a lot of the time we get beautiful clothes from stylists for a photo shoot. Then we find they don't fit so we have to split the clothes up the back to get them on.'

Now 43, Grant says the secret of her success has been to follow her instinct and not worry too much about the detail. She says: 'Sometimes you just have to go with your gut reaction. I think if you overanalyse things then you would never do them. Setting up your own business is extremely scary if you think about it, so I chose not to think about the money bit and focus on the positive instead.'

She thinks her enduring chronic asthma has also played a big part in helping her create a successful business. She says: 'I am not motivated by money and I have terrible concentration levels and a really short span of attention. But I am a bit of a control freak and I think it is because I have asthma.

I can't control the asthma and it flares up just when I don't want it to, and so I have got this need to control everything else. I am very tenacious.'

29

Gordon Montgomery
Founder of Fopp

The decision for Gordon Montgomery to go it alone was effectively taken for him. While working as area manager for Virgin Record stores in Glasgow he decided to set up a market stall of his own on the side selling discounted records. In preparation he started secretly buying up records from wholesalers and storing them at home. However, before he could actually begin running the stall his employers at Virgin found out about his plans and gave him an ultimatum. He could either forget about the stall and keep his job – or leave with 12 weeks' pay. Montgomery decided to take the money, and Fopp was born. He says: 'I had to think long and hard about it, but it is a great feeling when you walk away from a job. You feel completely free. It is a euphoric feeling.'

Brought up in Coventry in a working class family, Montgomery was the seventh of eight children. His father was a road builder and the family was always in debt. He says: 'When I was a kid I used to be told to hide under the table when the man came round to collect the money every week.'

Montgomery got eight O levels at school but at 16 he took a Saturday job in the local HMV record shop and halfway through his A levels abandoned school to work there full time. When his father walked out of the family home, Montgomery left a week later to live in a bedsit. He says: 'I couldn't take it any more, there were four of us in one bedroom in two sets of bunk beds.'

Constantly broke, Montgomery decided the only way to get more money was to be promoted. He applied for every job that came up and when both the manager and assistant manager of the store where he worked left unexpectedly he was appointed temporary manager at the age of 17.

When a new manager was appointed, however, Montgomery did not get on with him and left to work at the local Virgin music store instead. He spent the next few years working in different Virgin stores around the country and quickly rose through the ranks before leaving to go it alone with his market stall.

His euphoria on giving it all up to run a market stall was, however, short-lived. Montgomery says: 'The first day I took £13 and felt depressed. I had been taking home £200 a week at Virgin but I was making £75 a week from the stall. It was not enough to feed myself and my partner, who found out she was pregnant just after I left my job. It was a real struggle. I really regretted leaving my job.'

In an effort to boost sales, Montgomery started selling new releases alongside discounted records and took on a second stall. He began to carve himself a niche in the local area by selling records people could not easily get in other shops, such as ones by little known bands put out by independent labels, and imported jazz and soul recordings. He also sold mainstream records at lower prices than his competitors, which he managed to get from middlemen happy to offload excess stock. He says: 'I still wanted a bit of the middle market because it was passing my front door. You don't turn people down if they ask for Shakin' Stevens.'

After two years, however, Montgomery decided he might make more money with a proper shop. So he took a lease on a place below a Chinese restaurant, selling mostly punk, soul and jazz records.

The shop itself was a big success, immediately selling three times the number of records the stalls had. Montgomery says:

Fact file

Date of birth: 9 March 1957

Marital status: divorced with two children

Qualifications: eight O levels

Interests: playing football

Personal philosophy: 'You can overcome most problems if you look at them from a different angle.'

'We aimed at those people who have to be in record shops week in week out.' He called the shops Fopp after a track by a group called the Ohio Brothers and because it rhymed with pop, hip hop and bebop.

However, taking on the lease turned out to be an expensive mistake. He says: 'I was desperate to get a shop so I took over a lease which had six years left. But I didn't realise that at the end of the lease I would be responsible for all the repairs and maintenance of the building, which was in a state of dilapidation. There would be urine coming down the walls from the Chinese restaurant upstairs because their toilets would flood all the time. I arrived one morning and the whole floor was covered in it.' In the end Montgomery had to pay £40,000 for the cost of repairs and only managed to find the money when the bank agreed to extend his overdraft.

Montgomery hit another setback when he opened a second shop in Edinburgh. He says: 'I tried to copy what I had done in Glasgow but it took a long time to establish itself and was a complete failure for the first year. It lost money for the first 15 months but I didn't have the money to advertise it so I just had to sit tight and wait for the reputation to build. I used to get very depressed about it.'

However, he persevered and eventually the Edinburgh store started to make money, encouraging him to open another three stores. Each time Montgomery chose slightly offbeat sites and spent little on advertising the new stores, relying on word of mouth to push demand instead. He says: 'I couldn't afford the prime sites where HMV or Virgin open stores so I took quirky little ones and waited for them to build.'

The quirky image is one he has been happy to foster. He says: 'We are particularly good at selling CDs to people which they didn't intend to buy. They may not be familiar with a particular artist but they will buy it because it is only three quid. Then it gathers momentum and before you know it, someone is a fan. We are like a 1970s record store fast forwarded into the new century.'

In the mid-1990s, however, a crisis in his personal life threatened to derail the business. Montgomery explains: 'My wife wanted to move back to Coventry to be near her family. I liked living in Glasgow but I didn't want to be an estranged father so we moved to Royal Leamington Spa. I opened a little shop there and started to expand the business in England. But my wife didn't want me to do that and wanted me to spend less time at work. But a business is like a juggernaut – if you stop it is bound to go the other way at some point.'

He says: 'I tried to reason with her but then I did something bad. I did a deal to open a store in Sheffield and didn't inform her. She found out about it and we ended up at loggerheads.'

They split up and Montgomery found himself back living in a bedsit again.

He eventually decided to form a limited company to spread the risk and ownership of the business with three Fopp directors, keeping a 60 per cent share for himself. The business now has 25 shops, and in 2006 is expected to have a turnover of around £38 million.

Now 49, Montgomery says he is always thinking up ideas for new businesses but that 'most of them are useless'. He says: 'I once told my son that when I retire I might go down to the south coast and open a milk bar, because I like milk bars but there aren't many around anymore. That way I would just have that one business to run. I could go to work at 11 o'clock with a newspaper and see how it is going and then go home at 4. But my son said that if it was successful I would probably want to roll the milk bars out along the whole of the south coast and I wouldn't end up retiring anyway.'

For now, the record business continues to hold him fast. He says: 'My personal life is a complete mess but I am rather chuffed with what I have done professionally. I always wanted to build a business that had some substance to it. I have always been driven by the desire to succeed.'

30

Mark Leatham
Founder of Leathams

If you have never tasted Sunblush tomatoes or Camargue red rice it may not be too long before you do. For the past few years self-confessed foodie Mark Leatham has been on a mission to seek out fine food products from overseas and repackage them under his Merchant Gourmet brand to sell in supermarkets across the UK. He says: 'I am a born hunter and I love going off to find food which is different and to understand the culture and history behind it.'

Brought up on a farm in Buckinghamshire and then on a Greek island during school holidays after his family moved there when he was 13, Leatham discovered a love of food at an early age. He learnt to catch fish at the age of 7 and shoot at the age of 15, bringing home the rabbits and pigeons he had caught to be cooked for dinner. He says: 'When I caught my first perch and brought it home for my mother to cook, I realised it tasted better than fish fingers, which was my favourite food at the time, and I thought: "Gosh, this is interesting." Food was always a fascination for me and was very closely related to what came off the farm. From the earliest days, I valued the difference

between the wonderful food my mother cooked and the dire food we were given at the village school.'

After leaving school at 18, Leatham spent four years in the army where he spent some time serving in Northern Ireland. When he left he started shooting pigeons near his home in Buckinghamshire and selling them to local restaurants and pubs to pay for his cartridges.

But his father was not too impressed by his son's choice of career and so lined up a job for him in an estate agent's office in London instead. Leatham reluctantly took up the position but when the game season began he would go off and shoot at weekends, buying everything bagged on the shoot to sell to London restaurants. He stored the game birds in the basement of his girlfriend's flat in Chelsea, and would deliver them to customers himself every Wednesday when he was supposed to be out showing properties to sell.

Unsurprisingly, the arrangement did not last long and after only six months he handed in his notice at the estate agency. Leatham says: 'I hated working for somebody else and having had the responsibility for the lives of 30 men in Northern Ireland, I hated being an office clerk. If I was going to start at the bottom I wanted it to be the bottom of my pile and not somebody else's.'

So in 1979 Leatham became a professional pigeon shooter, supplying whatever he shot to fashionable London restaurants such as Albert Roux's Le Gavroche. His brother Ollie helped him with deliveries and they soon decided to go into business together, renting a former turkey-processing plant locally to process the game and venison they bought from game dealers.

Business prospered, and soon they felt confident enough to move the business to London. They borrowed £5,000 from their father to lease a butcher's shop in Streatham, in order to have their own processing facilities. Outside the game season, they started selling smoked salmon, frozen seafood and poultry imported from France. By the second year they had sales of £11,000 in Christmas week, the biggest week of the year for sales. They took out a bank loan to enable them to move the business to larger premises.

Fact file

Date of birth: 30 September 1955

Marital status: divorced with two children

Qualifications: ten O levels and two A levels

Interests: everything connected with food – shooting, fishing, growing vegetables, rearing poultry, cooking; entertaining friends

Personal philosophy: 'You have got to do something that you enjoy, to give you longevity in life.'

Leatham says: 'The years 1985, 86, 87 and 88 were dizzy years; any idiot could run a business. We were growing at 30–40 per cent a year.'

But in 1990 the recession came and growth hit the wall. Leatham says: 'Suddenly people were only interested in getting the cheapest price. As a quality food merchant, I found it really galling. It was a very difficult time. Like many people, we had not seen this recession coming. We had invested quite considerably in our future growth by acquiring small businesses, and by moving into new office premises.'

Leatham and his brother were forced to take drastic action; over the next two years they made 40 people redundant by moving their game operation from London to Lancashire and by closing down their smoked salmon production altogether. He says: 'I was flat on my face wondering what I was going to do. I was going into hotels that I used to do a lot of business with and they would tell me they didn't mind what the quality was, all they wanted to know was what the price was. Having supplied the smoked salmon for Royal Ascot for six years, I was told it was too expensive and that they could buy cheaper elsewhere.'

But by 1993, with the recession still in full flow, it was clear that further action was needed to save the company. Leatham decided that the solution was to switch the focus away from the catering industry and to start supplying his products to delicatessens and upmarket retailers such as Harrods, Fortnum and Mason, Selfridges and Harvey Nichols, where demand had withstood the recession better. He says: 'We found that there was great interest in the retail sector for our unusual Italian products such as porcini mushrooms, pesto and balsamic vinegar; they were fashionable and consumers were buying them.'

Then one day British Airways asked Leatham if he could supply them with some Camargue red rice because one of their chefs had put it on a menu and they were unable to track it down themselves. Leatham managed to find the only farmer in the whole of France who was producing Camargue red rice, the grains of which are red because of a genetic mutation. He enthusiastically started supplying Camargue red rice to delicatessens along with his other products. But it was not a success. He says: 'Nobody really knew what it was. It was expensive but it looked like lawn seed and it was sold in poorly designed artisan packaging.'

So when Sainsbury's asked Leatham if he would supply them with a selection of upmarket delicatessen products, he had an idea. He realised that the answer was to create a unique brand of his own. That way he could repackage all the unusual new products he had found in quality packaging under one distinctive label. He says: 'I had these wonderful products but nobody really knew what they were – and they were more expensive because they were good.' He decided to call his brand Merchant Gourmet.

Sainsbury's agreed to sell Merchant Gourmet products on the condition that Leatham let them sell his pesto under their own brand. So Leatham headed off overseas in search of more products which he could add to the Merchant Gourmet collection.

His biggest success was the discovery of some semi-dried tomatoes produced in France. He called them Sunblush tomatoes and registered the brand, and they are now Leatham's biggest selling single product. The Merchant Gourmet range now has 50 products including vacuum-packed chestnuts from France, dulce leche from Argentina, porcini mushrooms from Italy and pumpkinseed oil from Austria.

He says: 'If I haven't seen it before and it tastes good, if it's beautifully made and has an interesting story, then that is what gets me going. The ideal product is one that is unique, that is authentic and that is fabulous.'

Leatham spends two months each year travelling overseas in search of new products. The Merchant Gourmet range now forms a substantial part of Leathams, which has 130 employees and in 2006 will achieve a turnover of £32 million.

Leatham credits his mother with playing a key role in fostering his interest in good food. He says: 'She was always a stickler for the best quality ingredients, whether we were eating brains, chicken or fish. In Greece my mother would walk for miles to find the best olive oil or the best wine, and she still does.'

He adds: 'Everything I want to do in life is connected with food. I fish, I shoot, I rear poultry, I am a keen vegetable gardener, I love to travel in pursuit of food and I love to cook. What drives me is a passion for food. Once I smell something that is new and interesting, I go off like a bloodhound. As a small boy I used to lift up every bit of wood and stone that I could find to see what insects lived underneath and I am still just as inquisitive. But now I like to discover new and delicious foods'.